ABOUT THE BOOK

John Saul's long association with African countries, both with the challenges of exploitation, marginalization and dependency that confront people there and with their often dramatic struggles to overcome them (including the "thirty years war for liberation" in southern Africa), have drawn Saul not only to write widely on such African questions but also to reflect more generally upon the situation in the broad range of regions in the global South that experience, in shared if also diverse ways, the hard facts of poverty and exclusion in the present world of capitalist globalization. In this book Saul interrogates the reality of "underdevelopment" in such an unequal world, one driven principally by western power and capitalist profit-seeking and supported by inequalities of power and influence within the countries of the "Third World" themselves. Suggesting fresh ways to consider the dynamics of this situation, Saul also seeks to rethink the manner of linking a necessary class-based struggle with progressive assertions rooted in the demands of gender equality and progressive identity politics. In doing so, he looks towards a synthesis of democratic, socialist, and anti-imperialist sensibilities and invites scholars and activists alike to involve themselves in the kind of intellectual activism that can better underpin concrete and shared struggles, local, national, regional and global.

Socialism in Tanzania: Politics and Policies, co-edited with Lionel Cliffe, 2 vols. (1972-3)

Essays on the Political Economy of Africa, with Giovanni Arrighi (1973)

Socialism and Participation: Tanzania's 1970 National Election, co-edited with the Electoral Studies Committee, University of Dar es Salaam (1974)

Canada and Mozambique (1974)

Rural Cooperation in Tanzania, co-edited with Lionel Cliffe and others (1975)

Words and Deeds: Canada, Portugal and Africa, with the Toronto Committee for the Liberation of Southern Africa (1976)

The State and Revolution in Eastern Africa (1979)

The Crisis in South Africa, co-authored with Stephen Gelb (1981, rev. ed. 1986)

O Marxismo-Leninismo no Contexto Mocambicano (1983)

A Difficult Road: The Transition to Socialism in Mozambique (1985)

Socialist Ideology and the Struggle for Southern Africa (1990)

Recolonization and Resistance: Southern Africa in the 1990s (1994)

Namibia's Liberation Struggle: The Two-Edged Sword, with Colin Leys, and others (1995)

Millennial Africa: Capitalism, Socialism, Democracy (2001)

Africa: The Next Liberation Struggle (2005)

The Next Liberation Struggle: Capitalism, Socialism and Democracy in Southern Africa (2005)

ON JOHN SAUL
Aijaz Ahmad

John Saul combines in his person much of what is best in the international political culture of the Left. Canadian by birth, he gave much of his life to Africa, especially the Eastern and Southern zones of the continent, as teacher, scholar, sage, political activist, veteran of solidarity campaigns, and pamphleteer in the finest sense of that word. *Essays on the Political Economy of Africa* (1973), which he co-authored with Giovanni Arrighi, is still the seminal book on Tropical and Sub-Saharan Africa, with such classical essays as his "On African Populism" and "African Socialism in One Country: Tanzania." In his even more classic book, *The State and Revolution in Eastern Africa* (1979), Saul again penned several seminal essays on such themes as the postcolonial state and the revolutionary potential of African peasantries, while considering at length the possibilities of revolutionary change in Mozambique and radical transformation in Tanzania. Much of his written work is uncollectable because written punctually for small publications in the service of socialist solidarity networks, but even his recent lengthy essay on post-Apartheid South Africa, which he contributed to *Monthly Review*, is possibly the most instructive piece on that subject. The defeat of those revolutionary possibilities has forced Saul to think anew of the balance of forces in our own time, between imperialist globalization and struggle for socialism. This new book is the product of that reflection. It draws upon what he knows of Africa but goes far beyond that as well.

Knowing John Saul as friend, colleague and comrade is to know a rare combination of modesty and militancy, intensity and good humour, dedication to revolution and passion for basketball, wisdom of a life-long engagement with socialist politics and the clean youthfulness of commitment that lasts into old age.

* * *

More praise for John Saul:

"John Saul ... demonstrates how a flexible and non-dogmatic Marxism can bring fresh insights."
Jonathen Crush, Queens' University

"[Saul's] writings ... are all about instilling hope and learning from failure.... He is in a sort of underground, alternate Canadian tradition to the internationalism of Lester Pearson, Dr. Norman Bethune and Chris Giannou."
Rick Salutin, *The Toronto Globe and Mail*

"[Saul's] greatest contribution (has been) sharing ideas, criticizing and giving advice — reminding us that we should base our ideology on the concrete realities of our country and people, not on ready-made manuals ... that we should always ensure the participation of the people in decision-making, and make socialism not just a slogan but a real objective."
Jorge Rebelo, poet, long-time Frelimo (Mozambique) acivist, and cabinet minister in the first government of a liberated Mozambique

"A close engagement with the dilemmas confronting both leaders and ordinary people ... has been a hallmark of (John Saul's) work ... those who identify with their cause will find ... [him] provocative, sometimes uncomfortable, but always forward-looking and constructive intervention."
Colin Leys

DEVELOPMENT AFTER GLOBALIZATION

DEVELOPMENT AFTER
GLOBALIZATION

Theory and Practice for the Embattled South
in a New Imperial Age

John S. Saul

Three Essays
COLLECTIVE
Gurgaon

Zed Books Ltd
London and New York

KZN
PRESS
Scottsville

DEVELOPMENT AFTER GLOBALIZATION
Theory and Practice for the Embattled South in a New Imperial Age
by John S. Saul
© 2006 Three Essays

First Edition   March 2006

Originally published for South Asia 2006 by
Three Essays Collective
P.O. Box 6, B-957 Palam Vihar, GURGAON (Haryana) 122 017 India
Phone: +91 98681 26587, +91 98683 44843
www.threeessays.com
ISBN 81-88789-35-6 hb
ISBN 81-88789-34-8 pb

Published outside of South Asia 2006 by
Zed Books Ltd.
7 Cynthia Street, London N1 9JF, UK and Room 400, 175 Fifth Avenue, New
York, NY 10010, USA in 2006.
www.zedbooks.demon.co.uk
ISBN 1 84277 752 1 hb
ISBN 1 84277 753 X pb
Distributed in the USA exclusively by Palgrave, a division of St. Martin's Press,
LLC, 175 Fifth Avenue, New York 10010.
A catalogue record for this book is available from the British Library. US CIP data is
available from the Library of Congress

Published for Southern African region 2006 by
University of KwaZulu-Natal Press
Private Bag X01, Scottsville 3209, South Africa
www.ukznpress.co.za
ISBN 1-86914-082-6

Cover photograph by **William Gedney** (Courtesy: Duke University Rare Book,
Manuscript, and Special Collections Library. Special thanks to Linda McCurdy).

Cover and Text designed by Asad Zaidi
Printed and bound by Glorious Printers, New Delhi, India

for

Aquino de Bragança

in death as in life:
intellectual stimulus,
political touchstone
and friend

Acknowledgement: 'Dependency' [with Colin Leys, co-author] was originally published in D. A. Clark [ed.] *The Elgar Companion to Development Studies*; 'Globalization, Imperialism and Development: False Binaries and Radical Resolutions' was originally published in *Socialist Register* 2004; 'Identifying Class, Classifying Difference' was originally published in *Socialist Register* 2003.

CONTENTS

AUTHOR'S NOTE

This brief note allows me the opportunity to introduce myself to a new readership, and especially to the Indian readership that Three Essays Collective, the initiating press, seeks to service. It also is an appropriate place to thank those who have encouraged me in bringing together these essays in the present volume. Thanks, first of all, to Colin Leys my co-author in the writing of the first essay included here (as chapter one), the careful editor of chapters 2 and 3 when they first appeared as essays in the *Socialist Register* (2003 and 2004) which he co-edits with Leo Panitch, and my active partner in first plotting a volume along the lines of the present one from which he had, unfortunately, to withdraw his active participation (although he has remained ever ready to help, as an invaluable critic, with my present effort). I would also like to thank Barbara Harriss-White, another co-conspirator on our hypothesized original volume, who was subsequently instrumental in leading me to the Three Essays Collective; Asad Zaidi for enthusiastically welcoming me aboard at Three Essays in order to bring the present book to fruition; and Pat Saul for sound advice and support in her reading of its varied contents. I am grateful, too, to Robert Molteno and his Zed Press for simultaneously publishing this volume in order to make it more readily available to a "North Atlantic" audience as well.

While I am a Canadian who resides and teaches in that country, my main "Third World" focus in both intellectual and political terms has been Africa, especially southern Africa, where I have lived and worked off and on for a cumulative period of about ten years since the mid-sixties: in Tanzania, in Mozambique and in South Africa. I have published some fifteen volumes on Africa over the years, the most recent being my *Africa: The Next Liberation Struggle* (2005), and I am currently working on a manuscript entitled "The Thirty Years War for Southern Africa Liberation, 1960-1990". I was active for many decades in the anti-apartheid movement in Canada, discussing and publicizing the struggles for liberation in southern Africa, while also vigorously critiquing and resisting the often negative role played vis-à-vis those struggles by the Canadian state and by corporations based in my country; such activism included my serving as a member, for fifteen years, of the editorial collective of the Toronto-based magazine, *Southern Africa Report*. Having also taught "development studies" and "Third World Politics" for many decades in both Africa and Canada I welcome the present opportunity to share with concerned Indian readers some of my reflections on challenges faced, in the context of a rapacious global capitalism, by all inhabitants of the "global South".

In any case, the links between diverse continental struggles have, over the years, become quite tangible for me through constant interaction with others elsewhere in the "Third World" grappling with related challenges to those I was experiencing directly for myself in Africa. As hinted in chapter 1, the Latin American dependency school provided one point of reference for parallel African concerns that preoccupied me from early on. And I clearly recall the importance of Hamza Alavi's theorization in the 1970s of the "post-colonial state" in India and Pakistan for my own attempts to conceptualize the nature of the Tanzanian state of the time. So too, from the Caribbean, Frantz Fanon and Clive Thomas and Walter Rodney (my next door neighbour in Dar es Salaam) were stimuli to my perceiving more adequately Africa's own "false decolonization" and underdevelopment and their possible alternatives. Of course, the South Asian diaspora (much of it a reflex of Britain's [and Portugal's] enforced movement of people around its "empire") was also a constant presence in East and Southern Africa where I worked with such formidable African "Asians" as Tanzania's Issa Shivji, Mozambique's FRELIMO leader Jorge Rebelo and Goan/Mozambican scholar-activist and *citoyen du monde* Aquino da Bragança, and others in the Congress movement and beyond in South Africa who became valued friends and mentors.

But one knew of a host of other people who were also active agents, as both players and symbols, of the ongoing struggles in southern Africa: from Gandhi himself, trying out various strategies of resistance during his own South Africa years, to the many bearers of the messages of national assertion, non-alignment and economic planning from Nehru's early days. And, of course, further afield, there was Cuba in Angola and the impact, both direct and indirect, of Mao, Ho Chi Minh, General Giap and others that I was to hear spoken of so often by friends within the liberation movements of Africa's southern region. I was also to feel the links quite tangibly for myself when I visited places like Nicaragua and Cuba, and I continue to sense that such links are very much alive presently as friends report back from the World Social Forum in Brazil, discuss the strengths and weaknesses of the world-wide anti-globalization movement, and compare notes on "the struggle" in such diverse locales as South Africa, South-East Asia and Venezuela. In other books, as I have noted, I write principally about Africa; here, while directly referring to Africa where appropriate (in chapter 4, for example), I seek to present analyses and arguments that, I hope, will have wider import and perhaps even assist the world-wide struggle against global capitalism in inching forward.

INTRODUCTION
DEVELOPMENT THEORY THEN AND NOW

The extraordinary economic gap between the living standards of people living in the global North and those living in the global South is too well known to require extensive documentation here, although it is also quite true that there are inequalities *within* both the North and the South that must be taken equally seriously. Of course, the globally-defined and geographically-shaped inequalities thus noted can easily be understood primarily in terms of the imperatives of the present global reality. Nonetheless, it is at least as important to view the process of the making of this unequal world in carefully articulated historical perspective.

For, as regards economic development on a global scale, it is impossible to understate the significance of the economic breakthrough that occurred with the rise of capitalism in western Europe between the 15th and 19th centuries. It is, of course, particularly pertinent here to note what Europe did with the economic strength which the vagaries of history had rewarded it: in fact, Europe chose to accelerate a process of world conquest that had begun with the exploits of Spain and Portugal in the very earliest days of mercantile capitalism's dawn and that continued unabated as stronger, more fully realized capitalist economies emerged in Holland, Germany, France and England to complement, even displace, the centrality of earlier Spanish and Portuguese global assertions. To make a long story short, the rest of the world was subordinated to the economic requirements of expanding European economic and military might. As a result, by the nineteenth and twentieth centuries most of the global South had been battered and pillaged, and then, ultimately, tied to Western economic centres by lead-strings of economic and political (including formally colonial) provenance. A global hierarchy was thus formed, in geographical, class and racial terms that would have a profound, even crippling, effect on the economic and social prospects of the vast majority of the world's population.

One must be careful, as chapter 1, below, on "dependency" argues, to avoid caricaturing this global reality. However, as also confirmed there, it would be equally unwise to ignore it or understate its significance. There have, of course, been theorists, Rostow being amongst the first - although it is still the "common sense" of much established "economists' wisdom" – who have advised the global South to merely emulate the capitalist North in finding its way towards the future. Little if anything is said by such observers about the facts of a pre-existent global hierarchy and of differential market power (to go no further into the complexities of power) which profoundly constrain the prospects of those who must now try to compete from a position of considerable disadvantage with established centres of global economic dominance. For, as Giovanni Arrighi has argued, there is a

> seemingly "iron law" of a global hierarchy of wealth that stays in place no matter what the governments on the lower rungs of the hierarchy do or do not do – regardless, that is, of whether they

delink or do not delink from the global circuits of capital, pursue or do not pursue power and status in the interstate system, eliminate or do not eliminate inequalities among their subjects. It seems to me that a necessary step in the direction [of a plausible explanation of this] is to acknowledge that the standards of wealth enjoyed by the West correspond to what Roy Harrod once defined as "oligarchic wealth" in opposition to "democratic wealth".[1]

What follows from such an analysis? As recently as the early 1990s, Arrighi himself held that only a process of global socialist emancipation could hope to permit the development game to start over, with all players on the kind of equal footing that would allow the "wretched of the earth" to stand a fair chance; that only then could "a process that has developed to legitimate and enforce world inequalities be turned into a means to the end of promoting greater world equality and solidarity".[2] And yet, only a short decade later he could write (as also underscored in chapter 2, below), with several colleagues, an article[3] which restated firmly much the same carefully documented position regarding the dominance of a capitalist-induced, still largely geographically-defined, global hierarchy without once referring to socialism as even a possible antidote to the Western capitalist stranglehold on the global South. Instead, the sole hope for shaking western economic hegemony (particularly that of the United States) and global white dominance now appeared to lie, for him, with the rise, on firmly capitalist foundations, of China. (Note, however, that there is actually little sign, in his argument, of how the rest of the global South might benefit from the presumed rise of China [or at least the Chinese elite] within the ranks of the globally privileged!).

Or again, writing, almost four decades ago, with the present author, an article entitled "Socialism and Economic Development in Tropical Africa", Arrighi argued the unique importance of a socialist development strategy for overcoming the situation of economic underdevelopment in Africa.[4] How much more resigned, and singularly depressing, however, is his view in a recent article on the same continent: that "there may be little that most states can do to upgrade their economies in the global hierarchy of wealth", suggesting only that "there is always something they could do to increase (or decrease) the well-being of the citizenry at any given level of poverty or wealth." Conceding that even in such relatively narrow terms "African ruling groups have probably done far less than was in their power to do", Arrighi nonetheless concludes on what is apparently intended to be an upbeat note: "But it is not clear whether and to what extent they have on the whole been more deficient than the ruling groups of other countries and regions, the United States included. Indeed, if we take into account differentials in wealth and power, it seems likely that they have been comparatively less so."[5] But, even if this were true, it would still stand as pretty modest accomplishment for a destitute continent.

Such a defeat for the Left, such a sad whimper in place of once self-confident transformative assertion, may seem all too familiar in the face of the ever more dramatic ascendancy of capitalist logic and it is mirrored by the sharp decline of socialist aspirations in many quarters, finding particular echo in other writings by former stalwarts of the intellectual Left. Thus Perry Anderson, a brilliant analyst, and so often an editor of Arrighi (amongst other significant Left voices) at the London-based *New Left Review*, has himself shifted markedly – not, be it noted, towards any enthusiastic embrace of capitalism but rather (like Arrighi) towards a resigned acceptance of its apparently inevitable centrality to our world for any foreseeable future. Thus, as Anderson's biographer has recently argued (accurately I think):

> So while [Anderson] might sympathise with the contemporary
> anti-capitalist movement, he cannot conceive of its victory, [this
> providing] the sense of overwhelming pessimism that one gets
> when reading Anderson's recent work. It is to his credit, given
> this perspective, that he remains a staunch opponent of capitalism
> whose critiques of those in power repay reading by even the most
> optimistic anti-capitalist....[Yet] if Anderson's perspective is
> correct then the only principled position for a socialist to take
> would be one of stoical opposition to capitalism.[6]

Or to cite another example, from among many others that
might be mentioned, there is the celebrated Mexican Marxist
Carlos Vilas who once could assert, in a special 1990 issue (on
"The Future of Socialism") of New York's *Monthly Review*, a most
positive answer to the question he himself posed: "Is Socialism
Still an Alternative for the Third World?":

> But the choice for these countries is not socialist development or
> capitalist development. It is socialist development or capitalist
> peripheralization. Socialism is therefore the only possible
> alternative for Third World countries that are looking, not just
> for economic development, but for real and effective democracy
> as well.[7]

Yet, by 2004, his vision has become much more anti-climactic:
"Fostering representative democracy and endowing it with the
ability to carry out reforms and to confront the negative sides of
capitalist globalization and its domestic expressions are the most
that can be expected from today's progressive political or social
activism."[8]

In short, such analysts seem to be saying, global capitalism
doesn't work for the poorest of the poor, but, unfortunately, there
seems to be little or no alternative to it, with, at best, only modest
reform even half-way conceivable. In fact, without quite saying
so, Arrighi (and these others) are asking us to face a hard reality:
the extreme difficulty of identifying a viable global Left with a

viable global policy to counter capitalism and of establishing a global alternative with real growth potential and far more egalitarian practice to it. Nor do the essays in the present book presume to do so. They do, however, take the present inequalities within the world-wide economy as the absolutely central fact of the current global reality and also take the struggle to overcome such inequalities as the absolutely central challenge that confronts humankind in the new century. Furthermore, they take as an operative premise that such inequalities will, quite simply, not be significantly ameliorated within a global system defined along capitalist lines.

Is this global system, then, merely a bleak, inescapable fact, or is it rather a challenging, but nonetheless tractable, context that defines, but does not preempt, the radical challenge facing us today? The essays in this book argue the latter case, viewing the current global reality as, yes, extraordinarily hostile to the crucial aspirations of the many, in the South, who are at the bottom of the global scale in terms of both material conditions and present life chances. But these essays also take seriously such people's needs and, most important, their present and likely future efforts to redress the global imbalances that confront them. The terms for doing so – cast with reference to what I have defined as the three key angles of vision on the question: the issues of site, agency and imaginary – are explored chapter 2.

To take these in turn, the imperatives of thinking through more clearly who can and must offer effective resistance – the "agency" of progressive assertion – is canvassed. For many on the Left this has traditionally been seen as the role of the working class (or sometimes, "the workers and peasants"); and yet, although important, such categories do not always work so easily on the ground, especially when one takes as seriously as one must such complex additional realities of the real world of global inequality as the vast army of the unemployed and marginalized in many Third World settings – not to mention the differential oppressions of gender and of those of other distinguishing characteristics that are relevant both to the definition of under-development and to resistance thereto. There is also the question of "site" – local, national, regional, global – at which resistance to global capitalism can and should be best mounted, and, equally important, the question of how resistances mounted at these various sites might best be conceived, organized and coordinated in order to have full impact on the powerful global system they must confront. Finally, there is the question of what "imaginaries" provide the best integrative conception(s) – democracy? revolution? anti-capitalism? socialism? – around which to fuse diverse actions into a vision, a programme and a practice of effective resistance. Agency, site, imaginary: such, albeit in a preliminary manner, is the main focus of chapter 2.

As noted, I am also aware that one of the key impediments to establishing an effective revolutionary resistance is the diverse oppressions and the diverse voices that, socially and politically, have a claim to our attention – both for better and worse. For worse? One of the key factors in the remarkable rise of religious, ethnic-national and racial responses to the plight of the poor has been the failure (or is it the "defeat"?) of left-oriented, secular and quasi-socialist answers to that plight. Yet, as chapter 3 argues, such identities are not then to be merely explained away, for they have their own deep roots in social reality, even if diverse social circumstances can call them forth as operative political identities in quite different ways and on quite different occasions. Moreover, they are all identities (again, chapter 3 argues the case) that can interpenetrate with and reinforce more traditional left/Marxist demands and programmes (which is, be it noted, my own starting-point). This is especially true of gender/feminist demands, but it is also true for other, more strictly identity-based assertions as well. Of course, considerable ingenuity and creativity will be demanded of the left in seeking to articulate such demands (and to build on the resistances to real oppressions they often focus) within a properly expansive but also pointedly class-rooted, anti-capitalist, even socialist, agenda.

Finally, I have taken the liberty, in chapter 4, of drawing more directly on my African experience but also availing myself of a synthesis of my arguments prepared for a recent workshop, held, as it happens, at the time of my retirement from York University in Canada, which sought to draw together a range of scholars and practitioners, from Canada, from Africa and from a diverse array of other settings, to discuss a number of the issues which are also quite explicitly evoked in the other chapters included here. This fourth chapter is built around the four "background papers" which I prepared to help structure that workshop and that, to some extent, echo themes (and occasionally even quotations) to be found in my first three chapters; but they do so in an even more pointed and accessible form and with even more direct links to a possible practice of contestation for "scholar-activists" within the current global conjuncture. As intimated in my "author's note" (above), it is my hope that this final chapter, as well as the other three chapters that precede it, may be of some assistance in comprehending the tasks which now confront us, in realizing the kind of struggle (at once both intellectual and practical) which is so necessary, and in contributing to such a struggle's success.

DEPENDENCY
Co-authored with Colin Leys

Dependency refers to the way in which the "South" was subordinated to the needs and requirements of the "North" during the latter's capitalist revolution, especially through colonialism, and to the severe price the South continues to pay for the legacy of this today. As pointed out in our introduction, Giovanni Arrighi has even asserted the existence of a "seemingly iron law" according to which a country's location in the global hierarchy of national income and wealth created by imperialism continues to be the best predictor of its economic prospects, pointing out that the ranking has remained remarkably stable from the 1930s to the present day: "the nations of the world… are differentially situated in a rigid hierarchy of wealth in which the occasional ascent of a nation or two leaves the rest more firmly entrenched than ever they were before."[9]

At the heart of the dependency approach is the view that 'developing' countries are not just "behind" the economically advanced countries but remain subordinated to them by various mechanisms that must be abolished by radical change from below. Like any other term, "dependency" can be abused. Third World elites, for example, may sometimes plead "dependency" to divert attention from their privileged status and hide their responsibility for policies or corruption that help to keep the majority of their fellow countrymen in poverty. Nonetheless, dependency is a real feature of contemporary international relations.

The concept of dependency was first used by Latin American writers seeking to account for the fact that, in spite of having won formal independence from Spain or Portugal before the middle of the nineteenth century, a hundred years later their countries had mostly failed to develop into modern, industrialised societies. In the 1950s it became the basis of influential analyses of development by scholars such as Celso Furtado, Theotonio Dos Santos, Osvaldo Sunkel and Fernando Henrique Cardoso, several of whom were linked to the United Nations Economic Commission for Latin America (ECLA), under the leadership of Raul Prebisch.[10] Other writers have used other terms to designate the same general phenomenon. For example Lenin, writing in 1916 with reference to Latin America, called it "semi-colonialism"; Franz Fanon and Kwame Nkrumah, referring in the 1960s to post-independence Africa, called it "neo-colonialism"; while Andre Gunder Frank, studying the Latin American experience from the early nineteenth century to the 1960s, called it "underdevelopment".

In fact, Frank[11] formulated a general "law" of dependency, or underdevelopment, which held that the development of the west, the "metropoles", had been made possible by the subordination and exploitation of the former colonies, the "periphery", at the expense of the periphery's stagnation and impoverishment, and continued to be so. In Frank's view real economic development at the periphery had only occurred during the two world wars, or during the depression of the 1930s, when trade and investment links between the metropoles and the periphery were broken, or weakened. The solution to the problem of underdevelopment was therefore to end the condition of dependency through a revolutionary break. Other dependency theorists have advocated less radical alternatives, but all have called for a reduction in the influence of the imperial states and corporations backed by them – one or another form of "de-linking", "autarchy", or "new international economic order", etc.

The continuing relevance of the concept of dependency lies above all in the analyses it produced of the impact of imperialism, past and present, on the former colonies. Their economic structures tend to reflect the original reason for making them colonies: the production of primary commodities for export, and the creation of an infrastructure of railways, roads, ports, and telecommunications oriented to exports, not the promotion of an integrated national economy offering viable internal markets for more than basic goods. In the most extreme cases the whole economy may be based on the export of just one or two commodities (e.g. Fiji's sugar), and be extremely vulnerable to world market fluctuations or bad weather. The well-known decline in the terms of trade for developing countries is closely related to the unbalanced nature of their economies, as a result of which so many of them "consume what they do not produce, and produce what they do not consume". Moreover, the decline in the terms of trade contributed significantly to growing indebtedness, which eventually obliged so many countries to accept the "structural adjustment" programmes imposed as a condition of further aid by the IMF and the World Bank. Not only was this a new form of dependency, but structural adjustment also tended to reinforce many of the features of these countries' economies – especially their reliance on a few commodity exports – which were at the root of their economic difficulties.

Economic dependency is also reflected in the social structure. Primary commodity production in the colonial era was based on family labour on independent smallholdings, or on very low-wage labour on foreign-owned estates or mines. The typical result is, on the one hand, a large, poor and poorly-educated majority, still engaged in relatively low-skill work or, increasingly, crowding into cities with unemployment rates of upto 80 per cent, and still heavily dependent on domestic subsistence production by relatives in the countryside; and on the other, a small local professional and business elite, deriving its income from state revenues or from the intermediary tasks they perform for foreign firms and agencies – acting in effect as "compradores", so-called after the intermediaries in the Portuguese coastal enclaves in nineteenth century China.

This kind of social structure in turn accounts for the well-known political weaknesses of so many countries in the South.[12] Urban elites dominate political life, and the "civil society" institutions that are taken for granted in industrialised countries (such as trade unions, business associations, craft associations, nation-wide churches and national newspapers, not to mention democratic parties), and which in various ways make the elites more accountable to the popular majority, are often weak or even, in some cases, absent. Especially in periods of economic retrogression, such as Africa experienced from the late 1980s onwards, for example, people fall back on local and ethnic attachments, making national politics of any kind, let alone democratic politics, extremely difficult, and sometimes precipitating violence, civil wars and even genocide. As a result external forces continue to play a crucial role in determining political outcomes, whether by buttressing dictators, like Mobutu in the Congo and Bokassa in the Central African Republic; or by intervening to overthrow governments, like Chile's in 1973 and Iraq's in 2003 – or by declining to intervene, even to prevent genocide, as in Rwanda in 1993.

During the 1960s and early 1970s the most important debates about development tended to be framed in dependency terms. Three related issues in particular were hotly debated: whether dependency made development impossible, or merely difficult; whether or not underdeveloped countries suffered from "super-exploitation", as many activists believed; and what alternatives might actually exist to capitalist development, since dependency theory suggested that was impossible, or at least very difficult.

Frank[13] argued that "underdevelopment" (his term for dependent development) presented an absolute barrier to development. At the other extreme, Bill Warren[14] argued that capitalism would eventually embrace the whole world, ending dependency and levelling up living standards everywhere. Most dependency thinkers were unconvinced by Warren, but also tended to take a less pessimistic position than Frank, taking comfort from the emergence in the 1980s of the Newly Industrialising Countries or NICs (especially South Korea and Taiwan). Recent research suggests, however, that the circumstances which allowed these NICs to make their historic breakthrough were exceptional, and are not likely to be repeated elsewhere. A reasonable judgment would seem to be that dependency makes development very difficult if not impossible for most underdeveloped countries today.

The question of exploitation is closely connected to this. Many activists, especially, and in the North as well as the South, see the impoverished majority of the South as "super-exploited", and organisations like Fair Trade seek to counteract this. Geoffrey Kay,[15] however, famously declared that "capitalism has created underdevelopment not simply because it has exploited the underdeveloped countries, but because it has not exploited them enough." Two different senses of "exploitation" are clearly involved here. If India had the same level of investment per head of population as Belgium, so that Indian workers were exploited by capitalists to the same degree as Belgian workers are, Indian and Belgian workers would enjoy the same living standards. Today some levelling of workers' living standards has gradually been occurring as companies large and small move their production away from the North in search of lower wage costs. The impact of this in the South, however, remains limited and local, and the extent to which the living standards of consumers in the North are sustained by the low wages and prices paid to producers in the South continues to be one of the many unfairnesses (to say the least) of globalized capitalism.

The most serious problem for dependency theorists and activists was the question of what alternative development path dependent countries should pursue in order to overcome their dependency. Many dependency theorists, like the Russian 'populists' a hundred years earlier, have tended to advocate a return to some form of smallholder agriculture and local craft production. But as Gavin Kitching[16] forcefully pointed out, they have rarely been able to show – and all too often have not seen the necessity of showing – how productivity could be raised under these conditions. In other words, they have not shown how any development would actually take place on this basis, which has tended to make dependency an unhelpful starting-point for policy-makers and activists.

For a time some kind of socialist alternative did seem to be feasible, but harsh experience showed how hard this is to realise in practice. The distribution of power, both economic and political, in the contemporary world is such that a truly autonomous development strategy aimed at promoting the interests of the impoverished majority is extremely difficult for any individual country to realise on its own. Even a programme of redistributive state spending out of massive oil revenues, such as that pursued by the Chavez government in Venezuela, becomes a target of violent reaction by the possessing classes, with imperial backing. Many dependency thinkers now believe that the realisation of egalitarian development is only likely to be achieved if there is coordinated action on the part of a wide range of countries, and most probably only if there is a serious reaction against the logic and power of global capitalism in the imperial centres themselves – something not entirely easy to envisage in the short term, which is what urgently concerns the poor in the South today.

It is easier, therefore, to be driven back to a reformist position, hoping at best to shift the existing arrangements and rules marginally in favour of the countries of the South, to give them some room for manoeuvre within the existing global capitalist system. Yet no convincing case has been made for a genuinely developmental alternative to socialism as a response to dependency. True, there is considerable variation in the way different countries and regions of the world have fared under the burden of dependency, and in their relative positions within the persisting global hierarchy, as documented by Arrighi. But the burden of dependency is felt more or less everywhere.

Africa may provide the most striking case in point – of the starkest structural constraints of dependency, and of the inescapable need to draw on the socialist imagination in order to

overcome them. To be sure, Africa was perhaps the most economically backward region of any during the original period of Western imperialism, and some people still maintain that its historical backwardness has simply persisted to the present time. But this is to ignore the costs of the way in which Africa has been subordinated to the needs and requirements of western colonial powers, from the era of the slave trade to the most recent era of neo-colonialism. Although the concept of dependency was first developed in Latin America, it is unavoidable for any honest student of Africa.

For as Manfred Bienefeld[17] has written: "...both those on the right and the left would do well to remember that the present African crisis was most clearly foreseen by those looking at Africa from a dependency perspective in the 1960s... After all it was their contention that a continuation of a "neo-colonial" pattern of development would lead to disaster because it would produce a highly import- and skill-dependent economic structure that would depend critically on external markets and external investors and decision makers; that dependence would eventually become disastrous in its implications because the long term prospects for Africa's terms of trade were almost certainly poor; moreover, that dependence would be further reinforced because it would also create within African countries a degree of social and political polarization that would lay the foundations for an increasingly repressive response once those contradictions became critical. Finally, that view was also very clear as to the fact that this entire edifice was essentially constructed on the backs of the peasantry who would have to pay for it eventually." And, Bienefeld concludes, "This describes exactly the present circumstances of Africa."

Generally, it is clear that the price of the grossly unbalanced structure of wealth and power in the world continues to be exacted from those at the bottom end of the global hierarchy, through the mechanisms which dependency theory has unambiguously identified. Wherever else development theory may take us, then, it must begin by focusing on dependency and the forces that sustain it, and how they are to be overcome.

GLOBALIZATION, IMPERIALISM, DEVELOPMENT
FALSE BINARIES AND RADICAL RESOLUTIONS

The global expansion of European capitalism and the imperial conquest of peoples outside the western/northern centres of capital accumulation is a crucial dimension of the past several centuries of world history.[18] Moreover, the juxtaposition, in terms of power and prejudice, of "the West and the rest of us", of "North" versus "South", continues to have significant implications for the fate of people, and, in particular, of the poorest of people, right into the current epoch. This essay will concern itself with the question of how best to conceive, and to act upon, the problem of contemporary global inequality that has been so closely, if complexly, linked to the world-wide history of capitalist imperialism. Amidst the complexities, however, there is one thing about which there can be no doubt: that is the fact of staggering inequality and the sheer scale of grinding poverty that marks so much of the present global scene. Indeed, in a more humane and just world it would be perceived clearly for what it is: the single most scandalous fact about the current period of human history.

Of course, we may feel slightly overwhelmed by figures indicating that "a growing divide between the haves and have-nots has left increasing numbers in the Third World in dire poverty, living on less than a dollar a day" or that "despite repeated promises of poverty reduction made over the last decade of the twentieth century, the…number of people living in poverty has actually increased by almost 100 million [to an estimated 2,801 billion living on less than $2 a day in 1998]."[19] Similarly, it is difficult to register fully the import of discovering (from the WTO) that the average American earned "5,500% more than the average Ethiopian…a gap that will double in a century and a half at the current trend."[20] Or (from the UN) that "the world's richest three men have more assets than the combined GDPs of the world's 48 poorest countries" and "the 225 richest men in the world have a combined wealth of more than $1 trillion – equal to the income of the poorest 47% of the earth's population, some 2.5 billion people."[21] Nonetheless, on the Left, we do at least know that we should be doing something dramatic both to expose and to redress such inequities.

But doing what? In order to help clear the ground and to clarify what an appropriate answer to this question might look like, this essay will seek to explore a number of relevant theoretical issues. We begin with a critical reflection on the common tendency to offer diagnoses of global inequality in terms of false binaries – "the geographical" vs. "the social", "globalization" vs. "the state" (as well as "globalization" vs. "imperialism"), "development" vs. "anti-development" – while suggesting just how unhelpful these are in establishing a target against which progressive struggle can be directed. The chapter then turns to ask whether, even as we come to see more clearly what we are fighting against, we can also begin to define more pertinently just what we are fighting for in our efforts to overcome Third World poverty and exploitation. The word 'socialism' springs to mind here (not too surprisingly since what we are fighting against is indeed capitalism), but how far can this take us? For even if, as we shall see, the limited and contradictory nature of reformist alternatives presently on the global agenda encourages us to adopt a more revolutionary stance, there are real difficulties in establishing the precise meaning of "revolution" in the contemporary world. An inventory and evaluation of world-wide resistances – already the subject of a growing literature[22] – is beyond the scope of the present chapter. It must suffice here to identify some of the categories in terms of which such an inventory and evaluation might best be carried out, while seeking to suggest the ways in which greater clarity regarding issues of site, agency and appropriate imaginary could help facilitate the building and sustaining of a revolutionary project of world-wide dimensions.

I. Diagnoses: False Binaries
1) "The geographical" vs. "the social"
To start with: how, precisely, are the fact of imperialism as an historical phenomenon on the one hand, and the fact of gross pan global inequality as a contemporary phenomenon on the other, to be linked analytically? The commonsensical understanding of the existence of some causal connection between the coexistence of a wealthy North and an impoverished South that once structured many understandings in both left and liberal circles has come under increased critical scrutiny. There are the even more visible discrepancies of wealth and power *within* the countries of both North and South that must be accounted for, for example. Moreover, the countries of the South are now seen to be far more heterogeneous economically than was once supposed. Indeed, so

much less straightforward is a North/South mapping of inequality now said to be that a leading development theorist like Hoogvelt can suggest global inequality to be now much more "social" than "geographical" in its coordinates: "The familiar pyramid of the core-periphery hierarchy is no longer a geographical but a social division of the world economy," she writes.[23] As Arrighi and Silver have pointed out,[24] Hoogvelt's use of the term "social" is misleading: the geographical hierarchy of nations that they themselves continue to emphasize is, of course, also a social relationship. Nonetheless, what Hoogvelt underscores is potentially important: for her, a global division of labour, more centrally than ever defined along lines of class and (often) socio-economic exclusion that cut across national frontiers, has created both a dominant transnational capitalist class and vast outer circles of less privileged people, in both North and South. Such a model helps, she suggests, to comprehend both the diversity to be found in the Third World (stretching from the NICs to the most impoverished zones of Africa) and growing inequalities within individual countries – these latter leading, in turn, to "chaotic disturbances, violence and conflict in the [social] periphery."

But can we so readily displace from centrality the geographical coordinates of inequality? As Giovanni Arrighi has tirelessly documented (a perspective also highlighted in the introduction to the present volume), there is still a great deal about the global hierarchy that remains spatially-defined, and along lines that are also "largely a legacy of Western territorial and industrial expansion since about 1800." Thus, in a 1992 article on "the increasing inequality of the global distribution of incomes", Arrighi demonstrated "a major widening of the already large income gap that fifty years ago separated the peoples of the South from the peoples of the organic core of the capitalist world-economy." His conclusion (as already alluded to in this book's introduction): "the nations of the world…are differentially situated in a rigid hierarchy of wealth in which the occasional ascent of a nation or two leaves all the others more firmly entrenched than ever they were before,"[25] thus exemplifying a "seemingly 'iron law' of a global hierarchy that stays in place no matter what governments on the lower rungs of the hierarchy do or do not do." For in the absence of self-conscious correctives, the "oligarchic wealth" achieved by the West always tends to draw the bulk of capitalist activity towards it, hence widening the gap. Arrighi, updating his argument in 2003,[26] also emphasizes the extent to which aggressive Northern "neo-liberal" policies deliberately reinforced this hierarchy when, in the 1970s, things seemed set to shift slightly in the South's favour. He thus comes to precisely the same conclusion he had a decade earlier as to the persistence of a North/South hierarchy of incomes – and this despite (even because of) the fact that some degree of industrial convergence has indeed occurred.

It bears noting, if only in passing (see again, however, this volume's introduction), that the implications of the picture Arrighi so sketches have led him to make quite different responses over the short span of a decade. Thus, writing at the beginning of the 1990s Arrighi saw the on-going geographical polarization of global wealth as also linked to "systemic chaos", to "the continual …escalation of conflicts in the South and in the East", and to "increasingly intractable problems of world-system regulation for the West". Only the prospect that "Western socialists will join forces with Eastern and Southern associates" to facilitate the emergence of a "socialist world government" capable of "promoting greater world equality and solidarity" offered any hope to Arrighi at that time.[27] By the turn of the millennium, however, any whisper of socialism as best advancing the claims of "democratic wealth" against oligarchic wealth has vanished from his writings. Now "for understanding the present and future of the global hierarchy [and for envisaging its "subversion"] it is the continuing economic expansion of Mainland China that may be the most important."[28] In fact, this is the sole development, he and his co-authors suggest, that might have the potential (albeit one somewhat unspecified) to disrupt significantly the world-wide status quo. But note that this is a possible development that arises strictly from *within* the system of global capitalism.

Many will not wish to foreclose so readily the possibility of non-capitalist outcomes, of course. This is a point to which we will have to return. For the moment, it is sufficient merely to reject any implied contradiction between the "social" (read: class, and class-related exclusion) and the geographical dimensions of global inequality that the juxtaposition of Hoogvelt and Arrighi's emphases might seem to force upon us – and to register instead their irreducible simultaneity. Arrighi himself has no difficulty in recognizing the diversity of Southern capitalisms, for example, or the facts of income inequality internal to both North and South. But his continuing emphasis on spatial coordinates suggests the reason why notions of "the Third World", "the global South", "global apartheid", and even "the post-colonial" retain some efficacy in identifying the faultlines of global inequality. As writers like Smith and Cooper have observed, such notions can also be part of a language in terms of which global claims are staked and progressive mobilization is advanced in the South – even if they can also encourage a brand of "Third-Worldism" that (especially when manipulated by local elites in their own interests) blurs the inherently capitalist/class nature of world-wide contradictions.[29] In addition, any movement that seeks to unite anti-capitalist struggles, North and South, cannot ignore the extent to which many in the North have both shared in the North's 'oligarchic wealth' and been tempted by the racist premises spawned by the Western imperial project. If the legitimate claims of Southern peoples to global income redistribution, rights of migration, and freedom from high-handed military incursions are to be grasped and supported by potential allies of the South in the North, the latter will have to understand more clearly the facts regarding both the creation and persistence of a geographical hierarchy.

2) "Globalization" vs. "the state", "globalization" vs. "imperialism"
The temptation to falsely resolve "the geographical" vs. "the social" binary in favour of one pole or the other is in turn linked to another set of binaries that can with equal ease distort both the theory and the practice of challenging global inequality: the binaries of "globalization" versus "imperialism" (of "Empire" versus "empire", in effect) and of globally-focussed versus nation-state-focussed politics. Thus, it is no accident that Hoogvelt's "social" rather than geographic understanding of global inequality has been strongly influenced by the work of Manuel Castells. For Castells is amongst those who has most assertively argued the novelty of the current moment in the history of global capitalism, the epoch of "the network society", of "timeless time" and of the "space of flows" (rather than of places).[30] It is a world in which capital more generally, and the most dominant of capitalists more specifically, are said to have sprung free from their erstwhile moorings in nation-states and now dictate policies to all and sundry in terms of their now more forthrightly global interests. It is the world of Hardt and Negri's "Empire",[31] of Sklair's now predominantly *global* capitalist class,[32] and of a situation in which, in Teeple's strong statement of the argument, "capital [has] moved decisively beyond

its historic political shell, the nation state and its associated mitigating forces and influences...[as] the consequent growing loss of national sovereignty over social reform and government policy began to become displaced by the imperatives of global markets."[33]

There is something to this model, as thousands protesting against the inhuman toll of capitalist globalization have underscored in the streets of Seattle, Quebec, Genoa and in many other parts of the world in recent years. At the same time, as numerous critics of this particular take on globalization have observed, there is also something too neat about it – too apolitical to begin with. To be sure, globalists of right and left have underscored the saliency of emergent political institutions on the world-wide stage – the IMF and the World Bank, the WTO, and the like – but critics on the left have also been quick to point out that the system of global capitalism does not work quite so straightforwardly. Although capitalists (and their politicians) might be groping towards a kind of global "state", real states are still there to do a lot of the heavy lifting on behalf of capital. Indeed, so much is this the case for authors like James Petras that they feel confident to argue that not really much has changed: what we have is still pretty much imperialism – western imperialism – as usual[34]: in effect, the all too familiar realm of historical imperialism ("empire") rather than Hardt and Negri's centre-less "Empire". And certainly the recent activities of the United States (and its military) – now more active than ever, in the wake of 9/11 and with the invasions of Afghanistan and Iraq – as self-proclaimed global policeman has focussed attention on that particular reality, with anti-globalization protesters on the one hand and anti-war/anti-imperialist protesters having to work overtime to find an effective common language to tie together more precisely their obviously interrelated causes.

Leo Panitch has also emphasized the role of the state, criticizing much globalization literature for its "tendency to ignore the extent to which today's globalization both is authored by states and is primarily about reorganizing, rather than by-passing states".[35] In so arguing Panitch seeks, he suggests, merely to preempt any "false dichotomy between national and international struggles". Questions can be raised about his emphasis, nonetheless, for to some extent it could be taken to be quite complementary to the strong argument for the primacy of "globalization". Thus, the role for the state that Panitch seems to foreground is primarily that of necessary agent for establishing the parameters of smooth integration of the countries concerned into the global capitalist economy – including, at such states most assertive moments, acting primarily as agents for advancing the global aspirations of those of their own "national capitals" that have chosen to go "transnational" (cf. the Canadian case). At the same time, Panitch's argument is, with its careful balancing act, at some distance from a much more extreme form of the argument that insists upon continuing to see the states as crucially active agents within the global economy – that exemplified by Hirst and Thompson.

Still, in dismissing much of the globalization literature, even the latter pair of authors depict states as being active almost solely in terms of their ability to advance the "competitiveness", globally, of their own nation's principal economic sectors – presenting, in doing so, a 'refutation' of the globalization hypothesis that, ironically, comes close to echoing the position of the arch-globalist, Teeple, especially in its implications for the Third World. For even as they suggest the possible emergence, to frame such international competition, of various "institutional arrangements and strategies [to] assure some minimal level of international economic governance, at least to the benefit of the major advanced industrial nations", they nonetheless argue that "such [global] governance cannot alter the extreme inequalities between those nations and the rest, in terms of trade and investment, income and wealth." For them, indeed, "the issue is not whether the world's economy is governable towards ambitious goals like promoting social justice, equality between countries and greater democratic control for the bulk of the world's people, but whether it is governable at all."[36]

So much for "the bulk of the world's people", then. And just where does this leave states that lie beyond the pale of the "major advanced industrial nations"? For present purposes, one can even assume, with Panitch, that states in advanced capitalist settings do indeed have more room for economic manouevre than the strongest versions of globalization theory might seem to imply. And we can also acknowledge the importance in the current moment of one particular state, for clearly it would be naive for anyone not to give great weight in understanding the present workings of the global hierarchy to the role of the American state. Nonetheless, the possible weakness of a state-centric emphasis becomes far more evident when one turns one's attention to the *Southern* state. In this context, there is considerable cause for scepticism about the potentially positive role of such a state as an active agent of national economic advance, a reality that has prompted so astute an observer as Leys to write, in his seminal overview of contemporary development theory, that, especially in the Third World, "the era of national economies and national economic strategies is past"![37]

Of course, any such statement does bring us up, once again, against the fact of Third World diversity, from Asia through Latin America to Africa: it is no accident, perhaps, that Leys' major point of reference is Africa where he can list a series of measures that might, in theory, be adopted internationally to lift the weight of an inequitable global economy off the back of Africa and facilitate development while nonetheless concluding:

> The problem with such ideas is that they have no attraction for those who currently own Africa's debt, buy Africa's exports or arrange official capital-assistance flows. Such ideas could come to seem rational only in a world that was in the process of rejecting the currently predominant ideology of the market. While this world must come, it is not yet in place, and meantime the African tragedy will unfold.[38]

And yet, even if Africa presents a worst case scenario of marginalization and non-transformative exploitation under global capitalism, it remains true more generally that the strand of development theory once premised on the presumed viability of national capitalist strategies to realize an expansive form of development sounds, in the wake of the Asian crisis and the free-fall of much of Latin America, quite dated.[39] As the late Bill Graf has specified, "the Third World state is diminished, and more subordinate than at any time since the colonial era. Its elites are more externalized, and its hold on national sovereignty more tenuous than ever."[40]

And what of more left variants of the developmental state? The disappearance of most Third World socialisms (the "recolonization" of Mozambique, for example, so well described by David Plank[41]), and the apparent ease with which Mandela and Mbeki's South Africa and Lula's Brazil have been drawn into global capitalism's web, are not promising auguries here. Does this throw us back, necessarily, on a "global politics" as the key to unlocking the future for the South? Not everyone would so argue: there is, for example, Bienefeld's powerful claim for the continuing primacy within left practices of nation-state-centred politics. As he puts the point, it is because "of the total inability to conceive, let alone

construct, a meaningful political process at the global level" that
the requisite "global management of the competitive process, or
of a socialist economy, must be built on sub global units, namely
our 'generic nation states'."[42] Once again, it is difficult to avoid the
suspicion that this is an argument easier to make for advanced
capitalist countries than it is for those lodged more firmly on the
lower rungs of the global hierarchy. Still, thinking along similar
lines, Graf himself manages to conclude his negative survey of
the nature of the actually existing "state in the Third World" with
the argument that, nonetheless, only the state (albeit an alternative,
still largely "theoretical", state, in his phrase),

> ...can offer a feasible *agency* capable of aggregating the
> multifarious counter-hegemonic forces in the peripheral state.
> Only state-economic power in the South has any prospects of
> standing up to, negotiating with or countering the pervasive
> economic power of international capital.... No doubt too, only the
> state, in combinations with other states, can forge collective
> emancipatory projects directed against the hegemonic powers.[43]

Here he explicitly echoes Panitch whose seminal article
argues not only (as we have seen) the continued saliency of the
state as "constitutive element" of global capitalism, but also
emphasizes "the Left's need to develop its own strategies for
transforming the state, even as a means of developing an
appropriate international strategy."[44] It is a strong case, and all
the more so when one juxtaposes it to the rather nebulous and all
too unmediated politics inherent in, say, Hardt and Negri's
celebration of the "multitude" as their nominated agent to impose
a humane logic on capital. Writers like Bienefeld and Graf force us
to think more clearly about what are the actual mechanisms,
beyond the drama of the demonstration, that might be capable on
a prolonged and sustainable basis, of bringing real, effective power
to bear on global capital – and on the imperial (American) state.

And yet Negri and Leys are not wrong either: there is also a realm of global capitalist dictate that, through the actions of the IFIs and the WTO and international agencies and of the rampaging money marketeers and mobile investors, cannot readily be tamed by any one Third World state, however progressive, and that is not quite reducible to the actions of western states either, however important those actions may often be. The fact is that "Empire" (the world of capitalist globalization) and "empire" (the world of western imperialism) coexist: they structure, in not entirely coterminous ways, both the circumstances that produce global inequality (that is, the target of progressive activity for change) and the modalities of advancing such activity (that is, the most promising ways of "naming the enemy" and crafting the struggle against it). Avoiding misleading binaries in this regard, even as we seek in real and non-rhetorical ways to link both the global and the national (not to mention "the local", to which we will return) as appropriate sites of struggle, is one central thing that contemporary "development theory" must be about.

3) 'Development' vs. "anti-development"

Development theory? Here we confront another language that has conventionally offered itself to those who would deal with such issues: the language of "development" (as in the binary "developed" and "underdeveloped" countries, albeit often specified in terms of quite diverse notions of the relative importance of economic growth, the material betterment of people's lives, and more expansive definitions of possible human fulfillment). Since so much sound and fury has been thrown up on both the right and the left of the political spectrum around this term, and since so much confusion continues to reign with respect to it, it bears reflecting upon here.

Although not without historical antecedents, the "development project" was a product of the immediate post-War II epoch. It sought to evoke an "intellectual universe and...moral community" shared by rich and poor countries alike, built around the "conviction that the alleviation of poverty would not occur simply by self-regulating processes of economic growth or social change [but rather] required a concerted intervention by the national governments of both poor and wealthy countries in cooperation with an emerging body of international aid and development organizations." Eminently modernist (and capitalist) in its presuppositions, this developmentalist agenda (often articulated as, precisely, "modernization theory") for the 'emerging nations' was the Third World twin of the Keynesian agenda then ascendant in the advanced capitalist centres. The critics of this mainstream model were no less "modernist" and developmentalist, of course, with the most articulate of them grouping under the banner of a "dependency theory" which countered that it was actually the existing hierarchy of rich and poor countries that comprised the chief structural obstacle to realizing positive outcomes for the global poor. There were variants, too, within this latter camp, some more reformist, others more revolutionary and overtly socialist (along both populist and Marxist lines) in their orientation.[45] Still, as events would soon demonstrate, what linked together both modernization theory and dependency theory – the imperative of willed efforts to materially transform people's lives and the wisdom of utilizing the state as one key instrument in facilitating such a transformation (whether along capitalist or socialist lines) – was almost as important as what divided them.

But these shared premises would come under sharp attack from both right and left, a simultaneous assault that has created the murky terrain upon which (post-, neo-, anti-) development theory now finds itself. From the right came the neo-liberal "counter-revolution"[46] – one still largely ascendant in establishment circles – and, it would seem, launched as much or more against the capitalist theorists of Keynesian/developmentalist provenance than against any theorists and practitioners further to the left. This "ultra-modernist" project (as Cooper and Packard term it) was advanced in the name of the ever more extreme liberalization of markets and the attendant premise that, if only the state and the "developmentalists" would get out of the way, optimum results would follow for all, everywhere. Meanwhile, from the 1970s on, falling prices for primary products and rising prices for oil combined with the United States' new high interest rate regime to push many Third World countries ever deeper into debt and to make them ever more vulnerable to external dictate. With such political avatars as Thatcher and Reagan to trumpet it, the new orthodoxy of "freedom" swept through the IFIs, producing the so-called 'Washington Consensus' that became so much a part of the commonsense of capitalist globalization, especially in the Third World, in the late 20th century. For "free", however, read "free-market", the latter also presented as being the essential underpinning for the kind of "democracy" (best defined, however, as mere "polyarchy" or "low-intensity democracy") that such capitalist revolutionaries have also sometimes advocated. True, others have sought to wrest the discourse of "individual freedom" away from the free-marketeers for more humane purposes (Amartya Sen, for example).[47] For many on the left, however, it is the claims of the social collectivity (these claims being freed, to be sure, from the negative and undemocratic practices too often associated with them in the past) that seem most in need of reassertion.

The reinvigorated strength of global capital and the American state, as well as the neo-liberal ideology that has now come to epitomize their project, has also placed the developmentalist left on the defensive – as has the defeat/failure of socialist alternatives as economic strategies and as vehicles for democratic self-expression. In this context an attack on the pretensions of previously-existing development theory also sprang up on the left (broadly defined), often linked to the wider claims of "oppositional post-modernism", anarchism and environmentalism, and calling into question the "modernist", "westernizing" and undemocratic premises of the former orthodoxy, right and left. This is the discursive world of "development stinks", one that finds the development project to be an overweeningly modernist and Eurocentric project that also, in its emphasis on growth and participation in a wider global sphere, primarily serves Western economic interests.[48] In so arguing, many development-sceptics also underscore the extent to which the claims of women, the racially oppressed and the bearers of diverse cultures have been lost in the lofty abstractions of developmentalism,[49] and the integrity and positive potential of many local initiatives steamrollered in the name of grand theory and the disempowering centralization of many so-called "counter-hegemonic" struggles. Meanwhile, others stress the degree to which the language of development, with its productionist biases and its alleged Enlightenment arrogance, has blurred environmental concerns that are of crucial importance to the survival of the human race as a whole.

But even granted the need for such a sensibility – in order to beat back the high-handedness of often-Western-serving development agencies and NGOs, for example, and to ground our understanding of resistance to the inequities of global capitalism more effectively in the demands of diverse localities, cultures and identities – this need not dictate the abandonment of any vision of "development". Sutcliffe, for example, has argued convincingly of the need to bring environmental concerns together with a keen sensitivity to the facts of inequality on a global scale: "The conflict between the poor of today and the unborn exists to the extent that a real reduction in the negative environmental impact of the rich of today is not contemplated....Thus, human development is in danger of being unsustainable unless there is redistribution; and sustainable development is in danger of being anti-human unless it is accompanied by redistribution."[50] But this perspective has also carried Sutcliffe further, towards the strongest possible argument for the sustaining of an unapologetic (if circumspect) left-developmentalism. As he phrases it:

> The criticism of the standard development model seems at times too total. Because the old destination, which in the West we experience every day, seems so unsatisfactory, all aspects of it are often rejected as a whole. Along with consumerism out goes science, technology, urbanization, modern medicine and so on. And in sometimes comes a nostalgic, conservative postdevelopmentalism. In all projects, there is a danger of losing the baby when we throw out the old bath water. In this case the baby is the material, economic, productive basis of whatever satisfactory utopia can be, to echo Vincent Tucker's suggestive words, imagined and democratically negotiated among the inhabitants of earth.... One way of rephrasing all these concerns would be to say that development and globalization are experienced in practice in conditions of profound inequality of wealth and power between nations (imperialism) as well as between classes and sexes (capitalist class exploitation and patriarchy). It is necessary to distinguish which of the rejected aspects of development and globalization are inherent in these concepts and which come about because of the unequal circumstances in which we experience them. If we reject them completely because of the form in which they arrive we will always be struggling against the wrong enemy.[51]

This is a position echoed, in my experience, by a great many Southern social justice activists themselves, and also by such theorists as Cooper and Packard who, in speaking positively of "the marvellous ambiguity of the word development", suggest that "what at one level seemed like a discourse of control is at another a discourse of entitlement, a way of capturing the imagination of a cross-national public around demands for decency and equity."[52] Similarly Frans Schuurman, who professes himself to be "not particularly sensitive to criticisms raised against the concept of emancipation because it happens to be a so-called Enlightenment notion discredited by postmodernism", argues further that "a universal, yet context sensitive notion of justice is still far more attractive to reclaiming a normative and political progressive domain for development studies than any postmodernist-inspired attempt in that direction":

> The very essence of development studies is a normative preoccupation with the poor, marginalized and exploited people in the South. In this sense *inequality* rather than *diversity* or *difference* should be the main focus of development studies: inequality of access to power, to resources, to a human existence – in short, inequality of emancipation. There is no doubt that there is a diversity in forms, experiences and strategies for coping with inequality which deserves to be an integral part of the domain of development studies. There is also no doubt that globalization will contribute new forms of inequality and new forms of resistance. Nonetheless, it is inequality as such which should constitute the main focus within the explication of development studies.[53]

We need only complement such insights with Leys' more explicitly anti-capitalist injunctions – articulated in concluding his own impressive overview of the current state of theorizing about development, cited above – in order to ground a revolutionary left-developmentalism of great promise. As he argues, we must "revive development theory, not as a branch of policy-oriented social science within the parameters of an unquestioned capitalist world order, but a field of inquiry about the contemporary dynamics of that order itself, with imperative policy implications for the survival of civilized and decent life and not just in ex-colonial countries." Moreover, he continues, "if, as I fear, it seems that not much scope for change exists – especially for small, severely underdeveloped countries – without a radical subordination of capital to democratic control, development theory will ... have to be about this, and agents capable of undertaking it."[54]

II. Resolutions

(1) The limited variants of reform

"A radical subordination of capital to democratic control": this might be taken to represent a call to socialist revolution, a theme to which we will return in our concluding section. First, however, we must note that it has become apparent even to many of those who look favourably upon capitalism as an acceptable and defensible global system that, in its neo-liberal articulation, it doesn't work quite as well as might have been hoped, especially for the poorest of the poor. The terrain of proposed global "reform" of this system has been trenchantly mapped by Patrick Bond in many of his numerous publications.[55] I will merely note here, by way of summarizing the topic, three rather differing "reformist" responses from groups that have particular global resonance. The first group focusses on the social distemper (Arrighi's "systematic chaos") that this failed system has produced on the "periphery" – the fundamentalisms and xenophobias, the internal chaos and occasionally unpredictable dictators, that haunt such countries – and casts the resultant problem principally in terms of "security

concerns" (and especially the security concerns of the American state). Of course, the proponents of such a perspective do not view this as representing the failure of global capitalism. For the practitioners of this neo-conservative security doctrine (as exemplified by the current Bush team) are in fact devotees of the virtues of capitalism, their own ties to the oil, military and construction sectors of capital being well-known.

Moreover, when their house-intellectuals conceptualize empire in the language of security they also invariably make a heartfelt, in largely unexamined, bow to the virtues of "globalization" – with the global capitalist economy, as a kind of residual category, assumed to be churning away benevolently under everything else, its bounty to be fully realized once the various irrationalities of Third World politics are cleared away. For them, it is the peoples of the South who have failed capitalism, not the other way around. Sometimes this understanding is cast in quasi-racist terms, the celebrated work of Robert Kaplan being a case in point.[56] But whatever the rationale, the need to take action to impose order is the bottom-line, and the projection of this task can sometimes attain breathtaking proportions. Thus, for American security advisor Thomas Barnett, "disconnectedness [from globalization] defines danger": "Saddam Hussein's outlaw regime", he continues, "is dangerously disconnected from the globalizing world, from its rule sets, its norms, and all the ties that bind countries together in mutually assured dependence." It lies, in short, in "the Non-Integrating Gap", in those vast stretches of the world outside "the Core" which are simply "not functioning"[57] – and that is why war against it "is not only necessary and inevitable, but good." More generally, Barnett continues,

> a simple security rule set emerges: a country's potential to warrant
> a U.S. military response is inversely related to its globalization

connectivity.... [I]t is always possible to fall off this bandwagon called globalization. And when you do, bloodshed will follow. If you are lucky so will American troops.

Note, however, that it would be unwise to see the assertive actions taken by such proconsuls and ideologues of "empire" as being merely some direct emanation of the logic of capital. *Raison d'état* and moral/religious self-righteousness are important ingredients here in and of themselves and help determine that the kind of globalization they advocate – the brute neo-liberalism (paradox intended) of Bush and his cronies – comes most readily out of the barrel of a gun.

A second group of "reformers", perhaps best described as being, at least in the first instance, denizens of the world of "Empire" rather than of "empire" (although, needless to say, they are also strongly inflected in their policies by pressures from the American state and the interests behind it), are more polite and less inclined to favour the overt use of force. True, in practice they have been equally concerned to bat down, when necessary, the tendency of even the least corrupt of Third World states to intrude their unacceptable, "rent-seeking" ways into the market-place. But for them – and for the sectors of capital, in the financial, technology and industrial spheres, that are least comfortable with the hard-ball politics of empire – discipline in the interests of capital can be expected to flow primarily from the "invisible hand" of the market-place (a pretty effective system of power in its own right, of course). Much has been made of the shift of the IFIs, albeit more the World Bank than the IMF or the WTO, away from the baldest forms of free-market messianism. And one can indeed track the increased saliency of such non-economistic additions to the Bank's preferred discourse as "poverty alleviation", "local empowerment", "social capital",[58] and "good governance" (the latter, for example, seeking to recite the virtues of a more effectively "enabling state" as necessary to the facilitating of capitalist activity[59]). This battery of footnotes to neo-liberalism, the palest of reforms of the current system, is seductive to some, notably within the world of the NGOs, both Southern and Northern. But, in the end, such footnotes do little to qualify the extent to which the IFIs' still-in-place "Washington consensus" continues to see development for Third World countries as calling above all for debt repayment, the embrace of their "comparative advantage" as suppliers of primary products and a limited range of industrial output, and the rendering of themselves as open and attractive as possible to foreign investment. Just how much should we make of this distinction between Bush and the Bank, in any case? For neither possesses a vision designed to produce a capitalism any less parasitic, any more positively transformative, of the material lot of the vast majority of people of the South.

From within the camp of "Empire" there is, however, a third group, one which advances a more sweeping vision of possible reform – albeit a vision that, like the much more saccharine offerings of the World Bank, is primarily cast in economistic rather than security terms. Not that members of this group are indifferent to the various political "irrationalities" that now stalk the world of failed capitalism or even perhaps to the deepening plight of the global poor. But they are more preoccupied with contradictions felt to be internal to the capitalist accumulation process that the ascendant Washington consensus (whether dressed out in military mufti or in business suits) now threatens, they fear, merely to exacerbate. For they wonder aloud whether policies flowing from this consensus can really hope to maximize the system's drive to realize itself as a transformative (and, in the long term, ever more profitable) engine of expanded reproduction. As Robert Biel has argued from the left, the problem centres on the tension between short-term profit and "the long-term conditions (economic – the reproduction of labour – and socio-economic) for future exploitation." Thus, from the late 1970s on, protagonists of neo-liberalism developed as a Southern strategy the use of the "debt" as a lever to break resistance there to the demands of the new accumulation system. But this leaves a big question: "[Structural Adjustment Programmes] may have been good at destroying the old, but this does not mean they could provide a basis for a stable self-reproducing set-up even within the confines of the current accumulation regime."[60] For it is the virtual impossibility of the present system – now driven as much or more by the speculative activity of holders of financial capital than by the pursuit of "productive investment" – to act "rationally" at the aggregate level term that is crucial here.

Our third group expresses, but from within the world of capital, similar concerns regarding the current state of affairs. Master global currency manipulator George Soros provides an example here,[61] and Paul Krugman has also warned against the current salience of a "depression economics" wherein, precisely, the possible means to plan, world-wide, the kinds of judicious interventions in financial markets and other spheres that might facilitate expanded reproduction have been dismissed on narrowly ideological (read: neo-liberal) grounds.[62] Moreover, such warning voices can also be heard from time to time within the IFIs themselves with respect to the dim prospects for the poorest of economies under the pressure of purely market-driven calcu-lations: the views of Joseph Stiglitz,[63] Ravi Kanbur and Dani Rodrik have been significant in this respect (although we should also note just how quickly such figures are sidelined once the scarlet letter of Dissenter has been hung on them). However, even assuming for the moment the abstract potential of the model of disciplined capitalism that seems to drive such thinker/ practitioners, what is the likelihood of their calls for latter-day quasi-Keynesianism being heeded, either nationally in the Third World or more globally? Not much, one suspects. For, on a global scale, the prospects are not strong for development of the political mechanism that could impose the (theoretically) expansive logic of capital on the largely destructive (from the point of view of the global poor) activities of multiple capitalists in real-life competition. Indeed, for the foreseeable future, the realization of any very meaningful form of "global Keynesianism" must seem an even more utopian prospect than the realization of the least ambitious of socialist aspirations: actually existing global capitalism remains, as Przeworski once famously put it, profoundly "irrational".[64]

There are, of course, Third World elites who also play on the edges of these intra-establishment divisions, arguing 'the Southern case' for a degree of debt forgiveness, calling on the North to live up to its own pronounced principles of "free trade" (the latter's tariff walls often structured, ironically, to make the entry of Third World goods more, rather than less, difficult) and making the unlikely case for economic transformation based on more foreign direct investment. The response has been meagre to even the mildest of Third World-sponsored reform efforts by the powers-that-be in the global economy: the Doha Summit of the WTO in 2001 and the 2003 summit of the G-8 in Evian, France, are cases in point. So, too, are such items as the token Northern support for the Heavily Indebted Poor Countries Initiative (HIPC), the unbending pressure on Southern countries (in the sphere of "intellectual property rights", for example) to yield to intrusive WTO dictate, and the intense and continuing IMF directives against any form of control of exchange rates or capital movements. And yet, despite this record, initiatives like the capitalist-friendly New African Partnership for African Development (NEPAD), enthusiastically pushed by African leaders such as Thabo Mbeki (over the objections of many of their counterparts within "civil society", be it noted), continue to be offered.[65]

It is true that, as in the case of NEPAD, such assertions seem most often a ruse, their mild progressivism masking the deep incorporation of these elites (and their own class interests) within the "inner circle" of Hoogvelt's social hierarchy rather than representing any real attempt on their part to meet the needs of the masses of the population of the disadvantaged countries for whom they profess to speak. Nonetheless, many development theorists and many development agencies have aligned themselves hopefully with such initiatives and such elites (the recent move to the right of OXFAM-International providing a case in point). They do so, they sometimes say, in a spirit of *realism*: in order to facilitate cutting a better deal for the global South within what has become the only game in town. A grim and unpromising choice to feel compelled to make, if so.

2) The challenges of "revolution"

In sum, there is little evidence that the global capitalist system can or will be reformed in such a way as to deflect the spread of global inequality or permit any meaningful development for the vast mass of the world's population: instead, it seems destined to produce profits for the few alongside grinding poverty for the many. Nor is there anything inevitable about the overthrow of such a system. Indeed, as the morbid symptoms of its unchecked power multiply (manifested in the South, for example, in fundamentalisms and xenophobias of almost every variety) it is tempting analytically to see capitalism and barbarism as more likely outcomes, across the globe and in the foreseeable future, than socialism and development. Nonetheless, it is the task of the Left to make such an understanding of the sorry pass to which the world has come on capitalism's watch as much a staple of the commonsense of people's thinking as possible. And we must also ask ourselves, finally, just what are the counterveiling tendencies that might yet be expected to keep the struggle to transform the existing system of virulent capitalism on the agenda in the current period.

Perhaps some general direction can be drawn from the writings of Robert Biel, whose point of entry on these matters is close to my own[66] and is premised on understanding the present global system as one that has sought to establish in the "Third World" the ever more unmediated rule of global capital and the solitary imperative of capital accumulation. This is a system, he argues, in which policy has been downgraded merely to "a question of 'adapting' a country in the South to fit into the system by creating local conditions (for example, reducing interference from local bureaucrats) so that capital could find its way without hindrance to the most promising sectors."[67] At the same time, however, Biel suggests that this new system is also one that has created a fundamental problem for "the North" and, since it has placed the legitimacy of the Third World state under such pressure, this is true not merely in economic terms: "The 'national economy' is one of capitalism's best inventions because it provides a good basis for social control," he writes, and "the new form of direct rule which I am calling 'post-neo-colonial' [is therefore] very risky." As he then elaborates the point:

> The new vision may appear plausible to elites, since it presents the North and South as united within a single free-market

economic model (in contrast to the division between Keynesianism for the North and development economics for the South
which was characteristic of the post-war regime). But in reality
the free market is an expression of profoundly unequal power
relations, and the practical consequences of this are all too
obvious to the masses: to give only one example, it leads to a
virtual monopoly by the North of mass consumption.[68]

"All too obvious to the masses": would that things were so simple.
But they are not completely hidden from them either, as the level
of emergent world-wide contestation of the claims of global
capitalism begins to suggest.

There are clues regarding the possible nature of such
contestation in previous sections of this chapter, and other
pertinent literature has also been cited.[69] As noted earlier, I will
therefore limit myself here merely to suggesting some of the most
pressing considerations regarding site, agency and imaginary that
could help further define and advance effective radical resistance
to global capitalist rule. As regards the most appropriate *site*
(global, national, local) of struggle, for example, we have discussed
some of the seemingly unavoidable tensions that arise between
global and national scales in this respect, especially as regards
Third World countries. In the current epoch, the emphasis is often
put somewhat differently, however. Thus the liberal-left slogan
"Think globally, act locally" has proven to have considerable appeal
for those who seek to challenge the global system more fundamentally. For it is struggles cast in local terms against the most
proximate depredations – against the grossest of exploitation and
raping of the environment, from the demands of the Zapatistas to
the resistance to Shell Oil by the Ogoni people of the Niger delta –
of global firms, imperial states and their local intermediaries that
have captured much of the radical imagination in recent years.[70]

Such activities – "militant particularisms", in David Harvey's evocative phrase – are then argued to be the building blocks of the most effective of global assertions. Yet even if this is the case, it is also true that some brands of emphasis on the virtues of the local can be advanced quite negatively by the World Bank and its ilk as part of their highly suspect anti-state agenda. And a localist preoccupation can sometimes serve the most extreme versions of left anti-developmentalism as well, casting excessive suspicion on more large-scale, potentially hegemonic forms of anti-capitalist endeavour. Once again, the allure of false binaries must be avoided, just as they must be in thinking through the best ways of linking local assertions and national projects. On this latter issue, for example, South Africa's leading social movement activist, Trevor Ngwane, could almost be quoting the arguments of Bienefeld, Graf and Panitch as cited above when he asserts, on the basis of his own experience, that

> ...the issue of political power remains crucial. Some people attack the idea of targeting state power — the argument that globalization undermines the role of the nation state gets translated into an excuse for avoiding the fight with your own national bourgeoisie. But we in South Africa can't not confront the ANC and Mbeki. American activists can't not confront Bush. The COSATU leadership, the SACP, are happy to fight imperialism everywhere except here at home. Its been good to demonstrate against world summit meetings in Seattle, Genoa, even Doha, but there are problems with following the global elite around — it's not something poor people can afford to do....The point is, we have to build where we are.[71]

And, beyond the nation-state itself, there are also sub-global arenas of potentially progressive action, focussing resistances that manifest themselves at regional level (the African Social Forum, for example, and a range of parallel organizations in Asia) and even on a pan-Southern basis.

As regards the question of *agency*, those who most dramatize the purely globalizing nature of the current capitalist moment are also inclined to focus most exclusively on the sheer diversity of resistances – Castells in a wildly eclectic and unfocussed way and Hardt and Negri in terms of an almost poetic invocation of the awakening strength of "the multitude". Others approach such issues more soberly, while similarly emphasizing the broad front across which diverse identities (in terms of race, gender, ethno-nationalism and religion) and localities are both negatively affected by, while also capable of acting to confront, the realities of global inequality as they impinge upon them in the forms of exploitation, exclusion and the rampant commodification of basic necessities. This humbling diversity of situation is said to find most effective expression in a rich diversity of "social movements", with the latter in turn capable of comprising what Naomi Klein has termed "a movement of movements", the (loosely) collective actor that surfaces in Porto Alegre and Seattle and also feeds more focussed and cumulative global claims around issues of water, health, indebtedness and the like.[72] Certainly there is something to this, and, as I have pointed out elsewhere, Marxists and socialists would do well to heed the voices of diversity and of local definition of needs, possible modes of action and cultural integrity more effectively than they often have.[73]

At the same time, the celebration of diversity and spontaneity (the revolt against oppression but also against the undemocratic modes of political practice that is too much the legacy of the Left, not least in the case of various "Third World socialisms"[74]) must not blind us to the need for an increasing measure of effective organization and clarity of ideological thrust in confronting so powerful a system – especially since, at every site, locally, nationally and globally, that system can rely, when necessary, on powerful states to reinforce the irrationalities of the marketplace. Thus, as Leys has argued in emphasizing the necessary emergence, *qua* agent, of "unified" and hegemonic projects:

> Looked at in one way it will necessarily be a multiplicity of projects, in different sectors, nations and regions, [representing] the aspirations of different groups, movements and peoples. Yet unless these unite to confront the political and economic power of the transnationals and the states that back them, they will ultimately fail.... As a minimum it will require nation-wide movements and/or parties capable of exercising state power, and making it felt in supra-national institutions.[75]

Nor should diversity obscure the crucial importance of a class-based comprehension of agency, actual and potential,[76] including the key role that Southern workers and their trade unions have continued to play in keeping anti-capitalist and anti-imperialist themes firmly in the mix of global resistance.[77] At the same time, we should also avoid the temptation to abuse Marxist categories by glibly incorporating the vast numbers of the unemployed and marginalized that populate the South into the category of "reserve army of labour" in order to save the hypotheses of "proletarian revolution" and of the emergent movement's necessarily socialist vocation. As noted, such populations resist in terms of a wide variety of identities and grievances (even if they are also subject, in their desperation and in the absence of more progressive alternatives, to mobilization by the most self-defeating of fundamentalist and xenophobic ideologies). Nonetheless, some bridge to militant class awareness for the majority of Southerners might be found in the kind of expansive definition of class advocated some years ago by Post and Wright:

> The working out of capitalism in parts of the periphery prepares not only the minority working class but peasants and other working people, women, youth and minorities for a socialist

solution, even though the political manifestation of this may not initially take the form of a socialist movement. In the case of those who are *not* wage labourers (the classical class associated with that new order) capitalism has still so permeated the social relations which determine their existences, even though it may not have followed the western European pattern of "freeing" their labour power, that to be liberated from it is their only salvation.... The objective need for socialism of these elements can be no less than that of the worker imprisoned in the factory and disciplined by the whip of unemployment. These prices are paid in even the most 'successful' of the underdeveloped countries, and others additionally experience mass destitution. Finding another path has...become a desperate necessity if the alternative of conti-nuing, if not increasing barbarism is to be escaped.[78]

Note, however, that even the kind of "class consciousness" implied in this paragraph is something that must be won politically, not merely assumed.

And what, finally, of "imaginary" and the terms in which on-going struggles can best be conceived and advocated? An emphasis on the range of "disparate forces" and "multiple particularisms" from which more cumulative struggles of radical provenance must be built has placed the issue of "democracy" firmly on the agenda of the contemporary Left. Often the contrast with the past practices of ostensibly working-class-based parties and national revolu-tionary movements is self-consciously underscored in doing so. Moreover, the democratic imaginary will be especially attractive to those who must confront, as is so often the case in the Third World, the immediate reality of authoritarian state oppression (not to mention the lack of transparency of most of the global institutions whose decisions have such a pronounced impact on people's fates). This, then, is certainly a language of potential empowerment well worth clawing back from those, especially in the North, who manipulate it so unscrupulously. At the same time, any temptation on the Left to develop its project of resistance to oppression exclusively in terms of it – à la Laclau's notion of "radical democracy" – should be resisted, I think.[79] For, as important as such an emphasis is, and as responsive to diversity as any emergent movement for radical change must be, a project cast in terms solely of democratic claims (however "radical") is risky: it courts unfocussed eclecticism and a blurring of the target of capitalism, of global exploitation and commodification and of imperialist military and cultural assault that we know to be so central to global inequality and underdevelopment. Beyond democracy, "naming the enemy", at minimum, in firmly anti-capitalist terms provides an imaginary that is accurate and is, in any case, both implicit and explicit in much Southern practice. It also has the potential of driving an ever greater growth and consolidation of movements fighting commodification, fighting exploitation, fighting exclusion and operating at various sites and scales: "For all but a handful, capitalism has failed. For the rest of us, anti-capitalism remains our only hope."[80]

But what, one might ask, can this mean more positively, in terms of both vision and promise? Some have argued effectively the need to complement "anti-capitalism" with a militant demand for "social justice", for example.[81] And there is also, I would suggest in conclusion, a continuing claim to be made on behalf of the socialist imaginary – both as a plausible point of reference for struggles against capitalist globalization and imperialism and as a feasible liberatory practice for advancing Southern claims against inequality and for genuine development To be sure, the saliency of this once potent project has been downgraded in the eyes of many because of the internal weaknesses it has revealed and the defeats and/or failures it has suffered in recent decades. Yet it will prove neither possible nor wise for radicals in the South (or indeed anywhere else) to refuse, as diagnosis of current problems and guide to future practice, the promise of what Greg Albo has termed "realistic socialism" – a project which, in his discussion of the current parameters and likely prospects of global political economy, he has effectively contrasted to the claims of what he calls "utopian capitalism".[82] True, any such programme of "realistic socialism" will not be realized quickly, in the form, say, of some kind of revolutionary "big bang", as too often advocated rhetorically and abstractly on the left.[83] It will also have to be specified – globally, nationally, locally – not in terms of some pre-existing blueprint but by such social forces as mobilize themselves to place more progressive demands on the agenda. And, of course, it will not happen until even more people than at present, both in the South and in the North, embrace the fact that the existing market-dominated global order – driven by "a minority class that draws its wealth and power from a historically specific form of production" – is (in Albo's words) "contingent, imbalanced, exploitative and replaceable". Nonetheless, Albo's broader premise – that positive outcomes "can only be realized through re-embedding financial capital and production relations in democratically organized national and local economic spaces sustained through international solidarity and fora of democratic co-operation"[84] – seems a necessary starting-point.

IDENTIFYING CLASS, CLASSIFYING DIFFERENCE

There are more things between heaven and earth than are dreamt of in your philosophy, Ms. Marxist and Mr. Socialist. It's a critique we hear often these days from the principled spokespersons of anarchism, identity politics, oppositional postmodernism and "radical democracy", and of course there's something in it. The unduly heroic claims that some Marxists have sometimes made for the ontologically prior determinacy of "the material", for the centrality of the realm of the "economic" and the priority of class-based exploitation in explaining the oppressive workings of 'capitalist society' and the unnuanced manner in which some socialists have argued the privileged role of "the working class" (or, perhaps, "the workers and peasants") in resistance have rendered the Marxist/socialist tradition[85] vulnerable to criticism – if also to quite a bit of caricature – in recent years. In such an intellectual environment, it behooves Marxists and socialists who do prioritize political economy, the centrality of class struggle, and the realization of socialism, and who choose in one way or another to wrap ourselves in the mantle of the Grand Narratives of Emancipation, Universalism and quasi-Enlightenment values (even when abjuring anything that smacks of "Essentialism", "Economism," and "Euro-centrism") to think ever more clearly and carefully about the premises of our work, both analytical and practical.

To begin with, it is by now impossible to ignore the fact that gender is more central to how society functions – its oppressions and its resistances – than most Marxists acknowledged not so very long ago. But even as regards race, nationalism and religion we know – more graphically than ever in the wake of September 11 – that there are religions that move some people to sacrifice their own lives (and those of others) in the name of social claims said to be rooted in the imperatives of those religions; that there are nationalisms, supra- and sub-, that can drive some people even to genocide and ethnic-cleansings in their name, or feed the orgy of national self-righteousness that currently underpins U.S. claims to determine which regimes will survive and which are to be overthrown throughout the world; and that there are racist imaginings that, as in South Africa or indeed in the global capitalist economy more generally, can so interpenetrate with class structures of oppression as to make it often difficult to say with any great confidence which variable is driving which.

Moreover, anyone who has spent his life, as I have, studying – while also trying to help build – a political project around southern Africa and its liberation is aware of the possible flip-side of these variables, when the consciousness of racial identity and racial oppression can interact positively with the mobilizing and framing of class consciousness and class struggle; when, as in Mozambique, the emotive force of national liberation can provide the seed-bed for radicalization and ultimately, in however flawed and transitory a form, socialist endeavour; and when, as in South Africa itself, a religious/theological impulse towards liberation can be a key force behind radical undertakings. Of course, each of these realities is, up to a point, subject to a "material explanation". Nonetheless, there is also something here that can fall below the radar of the too easy reductionism of some kinds of Marxist/socialist endeavour. It is this something else, these provocative "disturbances to the field" of Marxism/socialism, that forces us to scan carefully the work of those who argue for the claims to our attention of the variables just mentioned – as well as the additional claims to our attention to be made in the name of gender, diverse sexual orientations, and even environmental concerns.

The aim of this essay is to register claims rooted in the lived saliency of "identity" and "difference" and, in doing so, contribute to striking a more useful analytical balance between political economy (focussed principally on the structures of capitalist exploitation that frame our world) and the parallel examination of other structures and other discourses that help define the realities of oppression. The essay will also suggest the circumstances under which class struggle can intersect more positively and self-consciously with those racial (read, at least in part, "anti racist"), national and religious impulses that, in some circumstances, speak to our common humanity and our common struggle.

I Marxism: "moralizing science", "point of view", "entry-point"

Let's begin at the beginning. Why would anybody want to identify themselves as a Marxist or a socialist in the first place? The simple answer is that we see capitalism as an inhuman and inegalitarian system of exploitation that needs to be overthrown. And what if we privilege this entry-point into social analysis in order to place at the centre of our concerns both the nature of the capitalist economic structure itself and the struggle of exploited classes to challenge that system? Need we apologize for the fact that this represents at least as much an 'arbitrary' value judgment as a strictly "scientific" procedure? For we don't need post-modernists to remind us that there are limits to the scientificity of the social science that we practice and apply. In fact, we don't need to dig very deep beneath the surface of "commonsense" to realize that the most efficacious social science doesn't merely drive itself but is framed by the questions that social scientists *choose* to ask. Recall, for example, that primary text of hard-headed procedural commonsense, E. H. Carr's *What is History?*: "Study the historian before you begin to study the facts", he counsels, for

> ...the necessity to establish these basic facts rests not on any quality of the facts themselves, but on an a priori decision of the historian....It used to be said that the facts speak for themselves. This is, of course, untrue. The facts speak only when the historian calls on them: it is he who decides to which facts to give the floor, and in what order or context....By and large the historian will get the kind of facts he wants. History means interpretation.[86]

And where do such choices come from? Not primarily, I would suggest, from some evolving and shifting consensus as to what is pertinent to the best "scientific" explanations emerging within social science disciplines (even if that can have a certain weight). In another fine old book of clear-sighted common sense, Hugh Stretton canvasses diverse approaches to the question of what caused late nineteenth century imperialism, concluding that even if his wide range of authors had

> all agreed to explain the same events and had made no mistakes of fact...it should still be clear that they would have continued to differ from each other. It should also be clear that their diverse

purposes – to reform or conserve societies, to condemn or justify past policies, to reinforce theoretical structures – might well have been served by a stricter regard for truth, but could scarcely be *replaced* by it.... However desirable as qualities of observation, "objectivity" and its last-ditch rearguard "intersubjectivity" still seem unable to organize an explanation or to bring men of different faith to agree about the parts or the shape, the length or breadth or depth or pattern, that an explanation should have.[87]

Indeed, Stretton concludes that "neutral scientific rules" cannot "replace valuation as selectors" and that the "scientistic" dream of developing an internally coherent, self-sustaining and [potentially] exhaustive model of society is not only misguided but dangerous – dangerous in the sense of encouraging a blunting of debate about the "political and moral valuations" that necessarily help shape both the questions posed of society and the explanations that contest for our attention regarding social phenomena. Hence his argument for the self-conscious embrace of what he terms a (necessarily) "moralizing [social] science". We might wish to add that, once the questions themselves have been posed, the social scientist can still be judged by his or her peers in terms of the evidence discovered and adduced in the attempt to answer them, and in terms of the logic and coherence of the arguments presented. There are scientific canons of evidence and argument in terms of which explanations can, up to a point, be judged "intersubjectively". But the questions themselves quite simply do not emerge unprompted from such concerns.

Although not always acknowledged, this seems straightforward enough. But even if some social scientists are uncomfortable with this notion of an inevitably "moralizing social science", the Marxist/socialist social scientist has no reason not to embrace it. After all, is this not what the unity of theory and practice is all about? This is the argument of Gavin Kitching, for example, who writes (affirmatively) that Marxism is much less a science than a "point of view", and, more specifically, a point of view "on or about the form of society that it calls capitalism".[88] For Kitching, "the Marxist point of view" (which Kitching himself adopts) turns out to be a *"rationally motivated willingness to act to transform capitalism"*. It has been, Kitching argues, "the "objectively best" point of view to take on capitalism ... *in order to change it into a better form of society"*[89] – and hence also the basis for the kind of politics of persuasion and mobilization of interests that could alone make the struggle for socialism viable.

I find this convincing – even though Kitching himself seems to take his own argument much too far when he suggests that, whatever may be its positive moral-cum-political value, the Marxist point of view does not provide any "privileged means" of understanding the workings of capitalist society and its contradictions. The truth is, of course, that Marxists and socialists seek not only to change the world but also to interpret it – and their central concerns have indeed given them tools with which to do so. Still, it is appropriate to ask just what, more broadly, is the kind of knowledge these concerns can produce. One well-known answer to this was articulated by Lucio Colletti in his widely-read essay "Marxism: Science or Revolution?"[90] Colletti focussed on the wage relationship within capitalism and conceded that "bourgeois social science" (as viewed from "the point of view of the capitalist", as Colletti put it) offers an understanding of that relationship as a free exchange that is quite plausible (and, we might add, fits neatly into the 'scientific' undertakings of neo-classical economics). But, Colletti insisted, equally plausible (and even more pertinent to the cause of socialist revolution) is an understanding of this relationship – "from the viewpoint of the working class" – as one of exploitation, and this angle of vision can also offer a revealing (but very different) analysis of the workings of capitalism.[91]

"The worker's point of view"? It is tempting to put it like this (not least for purposes of political mobilization), but we can actually advance the case for the prioritizing of a class analysis grounded in Marxist/socialist premises somewhat more modestly, albeit with equal effect. Indeed, Resnick and Wolff have done so convincingly in their volume, *Knowledge and Class*, rejecting both "empiricist" and "rationalist" epistemologies while announcing, unapologetically, that, as Marxists, they choose class analysis as their preferred "entry point" into social enquiry.[92] Interestingly, they make no claim that this is the only useful approach to society for purposes of theory or practice but assert merely that it is the one they find most illuminating to build from, both analytically and politically: "Class then is [the] one process among the many different processes of life chosen by Marxists as their theoretical entry point so as to make a particular sense of and a particular change in this life." But "why choose class as an entry-point rather than, say, racial or sexual oppression?":

> Our answer may serve to clarify our relations both to Marx and to those people today (including friends) whose entry points and hence theories differ more or less from ours. What Marx sought, and we continue to seek to contribute to struggles for social change, are not only our practical energies but also certain distinctive theoretical insights. The most important of these for us concerns class. Marx discovered, we think, a specific social process that his allies in social struggle had missed. The process in question is the production and distribution of surplus labour in society. Marx's contribution lay in defining, locating and connecting the class process to all other processes comprising the social totality they all sought to change. Marx's presumption was that programs for social change had less chance of success to the degree that their grasp of social structure was deficient.[93]

Note, in addition, that Resnick and Wolff see this way of expressing things as avoiding any kind of reductionism and instead as defining a Marxism that is open, precisely, to "the mutual overdetermination of both class and nonclass" dimensions, and thus to "the complex interdependencies of class and nonclass aspects of social life...that neither Marx nor we reduce to cause-effect or determining-determined essentialisms."[94] This latter point is crucial and we will return to it in the next section. But what, first, of the core argument I have presented regarding Marxism's scientific-cum-political standing – as "moralizing science", as "point of view", as "entry-point" – to our analytical understandings? No doubt philosophers, including Marxist philosophers, may wish to go further than this, but I'm not sure that the rest of us can't get on with our own work while they're doing so. Isn't this approach, in any case, the best way to stake our claim to be heard, to mobilize and expand our constituency for class analysis and class struggle, while also listening carefully to what others struggling alongside us have to say?

As for the post-Marxist and post-modernist sages, can we not safely leave them to recycling such assertions as that of Ernesto Laclau to the effect that "class struggle is just one species of identity politics, and one which is becoming less and less important in the world in which we live." No doubt Laclau's attendant claim that class struggle is hopelessly "old fashioned" will be good news to the transnational corporations and the IFIs and the US State Department that drive the global economy – although they might be inclined to see this more as a whimper of defeat than a theoretical breakthrough. For Laclau's statement is linked in his text to a broader approach that characterizes "anti-capitalism" as "mere empty talk", the goal of socializing the means of production as a "rather peculiar aim", and the height of left aspirations as just enough reform of the economy so that "the worst effects of globalization are avoided".[95] As Slavoj Zizek suggests (in critiquing Laclau), such a refusal to "even imagine a viable alternative to global capitalism" inevitably produces the conclusion that "the only option for the Left is ... palliative measures which, while resigning themselves to the course of events, restrict themselves to limiting the damaging effects of the inevitable."[96]

But let us be generous and also say to the "posties": go ahead, "deconstruct" us to your heart's content, expose our premises (our Eurocentrisms, essentialisms and the like) and we're prepared to learn from you just where we may have occluded things, thereby bettering both our science (our "moralizing science") and our politics. At the end of the day, however, Marxists and socialists will also continue to insist that capitalism be taken seriously in its fundamentally oppressive reality – and to insist as well that, like all human constructs, it is not destined to last forever but can and must be replaced as soon as possible. And to assert that mobilizing people who are victims of that system around anti-capitalist themes and projects is essential to liberation. And to ask of others why they would want, in all conscience, to blunt that "point-of-view".

II Marxism: Anti-Reductionist and Non-Essentialist

This, then, is our entry-point: we begin as Marxists with capitalism itself because we consider an understanding of its logic to be the crucial first step in our understanding of the world, and we begin as socialists with the struggle to overthrow capitalism because we consider that overthrow to be a necessary (if not sufficient) condition of human emancipation. From this affirmation we can now return to the issues raised in our introductory paragraphs: following Resnick and Wolf, I will argue that there is simply no need, either theoretically or politically, for Marxists/socialists to downplay the importance of other kinds of oppression or other kinds of meaningful resistance to such oppressions.

For despite all the huffing and puffing over the past couple of decades by so many post-Marxists, post-structuralists and post-modernists, Marxism has the resources to deal with a complete plate-full of "differences" and to keep its honour bright. Once again, Kitching has effectively phrased the point:

> Marx simply was *not* an economic reductionist. He did not believe that all forms of politics, or culture, or social conflict were simply expressions of underlying economic or class interests, and it would be extremely difficult to find any evidence in his writing that he did....Marx was often concerned with those *aspects* of politics, or culture, or social conflict that had class or economic dimensions. But he certainly would not have thought that, for example, all classical Greek culture (which he loved) or all the politics of the French Second Empire (by which he was fascinated) could be explained by or reduced to economic or class factors.[97]

Of course, there are tensions within Marx's work (and also within the tradition he spawned): he did want to say that the production process – and the capitalist production process in particular – was a (sometimes, "the") crucial variable for framing both social analysis and political practice. And there are those who will continue to argue, albeit in subtle ways, the case for the *primacy* of the "economic" and of class struggle. Take, for example, the position asserted some years ago by Erik Olin Wright. He sought to sustain such a claim on the grounds that a tendency towards transformation of the class struggle is inherent in the very process of economic development (in the development of the productive forces), providing class relations with an "internal logic of development" denied to other forms of domination: "the apparent symmetry in the relationship between class and gender or class and race, therefore, is disrupted by the developmental tendencies of class relations. No such developmental trajectory has been persuasively argued for other forms of domination," Wright asserted.[98] Suggestive, but even then probably more reductionist than it need be. Not that "suggestive" is a bad thing: the pull towards economic-cum-class reductionism within Marxism can be illuminating, even if also dangerous.

But dangerous? This need prove to be the case only if we fail to hold onto the expansive implications of the simultaneous pull towards "agency" within Marxism.[99] "Man [sic] makes his own history but he does not do so under conditions of his own choosing": a phrase from Marx that is often quoted but perhaps too easily forgotten. For if we take this (usefully contradictory) phrase seriously, we are acknowledging that there do exist tensions within our approach: tensions between structure and agency, tensions between the attractions of economic-cum-class reductionism (in both analysis and politics) on the one hand and the legitimate claims of a multi-variate analysis and a politically inclusive approach to struggle on the other. What we are then claiming is that it is precisely on the cusp of these tensions that the Marxist chooses, as creatively and self-consciously as possible, to think and to act.

In fact, we need only build on the possibilities (tensions) inherent in one of Marx's own most tantalizing formulations:

> It is always the direct relationship of the owners of the conditions of production to the direct producers – a relationship always naturally corresponding to the development of the methods of labour and thereby its social productivity – which reveals the innermost secret, the hidden basis of the entire social structure, and with it the political form of the relation of sovereignty and dependence, in short, the corresponding specific form of the state. This does not prevent the same economic basis – the same from the standpoint of its main conditions – due to innumerable

> different empirical circumstances, natural environment, race
> relations, external historical influences, etc., from showing infinite
> variations and gradations in appearance, which can be ascer-
> tained only by analysis of the empirically given circumstances.[100]

The absence of any mention of gender on Marx's list (or, one might
add, of sexual orientation, religion or ethno-nationalism) is trou-
bling, to be sure, and there is the word "appearance" to be dealt
with. And yet, merely expand the content of that "etc." and of those
phrases "empirical circumstances" and "external historical influences", while also interpreting "appearance" in the strongest
possible sense (as capable of housing pertinent effects in its own
right), and you have pretty much all that Marxists require: the
ability to emphasize the production process as our chosen entry-
point into social analysis and political practice while also taking
seriously the concerns of those who wish to highlight, alterna-
tively or simultaneously, the claims to our attention of other nodes
of oppression and resistance. This done, all that Marxists need
ask of those who speak out analytically and politically from the
vantage-point of concern about these is that, whatever else they
do, they take seriously the goal of overthrowing, sooner or later
(but preferably sooner rather than later), the capitalist system.

Although their efforts are not the immediate focus of this
essay, it bears emphasizing that it has been those engaged in
gender-sensitive analysis and feminist struggles who have had
most to contribute to the development of Marxist analysis along
these expansive lines. This can be seen firstly with reference to the
very notion of class itself. Himani Bannerji has underscored the
"absurdity" of attempting to see "identity and difference as
historical forms of consciousness unconnected to class formation,
development of capital and class politics." But in doing so she also
emphasizes the impossibility of considering class itself outside
the gendering (and "race-ing") that so often significantly

characterize it in the concrete.[101] Not that there need be anything so very startling in this. Katha Pollitt makes the relevant point about the United States (but the point is true more generally) in answering her own question: "Are race and gender and sexual orientation distractions from basic issues of economic inequality and social class?"

> All you have to do is look squarely at the world you live in and it is perfectly obvious that ... race and gender are crucial means through which class is structured. These are not side issues that can be resolved by raising the minimum wage, although that is important, or even by unionizing more workplaces, although that is important too. Inequality in America is too solidly based on racism and sexism for it be altered without acknowledging race, and sex and sexuality.[102]

But this point can also be turned around, underscoring the extent to which gender oppression is also classed and the extent to which feminist assertions must interpenetrate with socialist ones in order to be pertinent to the life-conditions of most women. As Lynn Segal argued a decade ago, "at a time when the advances made by some women are so clearly overshadowed by the increasing poverty experienced so acutely by others (alongside the unemployment of men of their class and group) it seems perverse to pose women's specific interests against rather than alongside more traditional socialist goals."[103] Consider, too, Nancy Fraser's twin framing of the conditions of women's oppression (and a number of other oppressions as well) within the spheres of both distribution *and* difference: "Demands for 'recognition of difference' fuel struggles of groups mobilized under the banners of nationality, ethnicity, 'race', gender, and sexuality. In these 'post-socialist' conflicts, group identity supplants class interest as the chief medium of political mobilization. And cultural recognition displaces socioeconomic redistribution as the remedy for injustice and the goal of political struggle."[104] And yet, she then argues, it seems extremely unlikely that tensions rooted in struggles for "recognition" can be resolved, in the long-term, in any very effective and healing manner unless tensions rooted in struggles for "redistribution" (broadly defined) are also being addressed. Her own aim, she suggests, is precisely "to connect two political problematics that are currently dissociated from one another."

True, Fraser casts her concern for the economic in narrowly redistributional terms rather than in terms of overcoming capitalism's class oppressions more radically. Nonetheless, her refusal to let feminist scholarship and practice merely disappear into the morass of "difference" and discourse theory is a bracing one. Moreover, other, more Marxist feminists have been prepared to take the point much further in viewing "feminist struggle" as "fundamentally a class war over resources, knowledge and power" and in seeking to "reclaim anticapitalist feminism". Thus Hennessy and Ingraham bemoan the fact that "debate among first-world socialist and marxist feminists has drifted so far into theorizing women's oppression in terms of culture, consciousness and ideology that concerns over how to explain the connection between patriarchy and capitalism, or the links between women's domestic labour and ideology, have been all but abandoned."[105] In contrast, as they and their co-authors have demonstrated in their work, a preoccupation with the mode of production and with the realities of wage labour, commodity production and consumption is crucial both to "the scientific understanding of sexual inequality" and to feminists gaining "a sound basis for the evaluation of short- and long-term political and economic objectives."[106]

Such a position is, of course, not seen as pre-empting the claims of anti-patriarchal struggle as carried out "in its own right". It is a commonplace, albeit a crucial one, that a "mere" overthrow of capitalism will not, in and of itself, resolve the issues of oppressive sexism and gender emancipation (issues that have continued to haunt all previous experiments in socialist construction). As Hennessy and Ingraham are quick to acknowledge, "violations of women's needs and rights as human beings by patriarchal practices like rape, battering, clitoridectomy and other forms of sexual violence, as well as the neglect and infanticide of girls, are not exclusively bound by or peculiar to capitalism." But they do assert that "the historical forms these practices take and their use against many women in the world are not independent of capitalism either," concluding that "because marxist feminists see the continuous historical connections between women's oppression and capitalism, theirs is a politics of social transformation that ultimately looks to the elimination of class."[107] Indeed as Hennessy – in articulating her own commitment, as socialist, feminist and lesbian activist, to Marxist analysis and politics – concludes another recent study: "Full democracy [deemed by her to be essential to, amongst many other things, sexual emancipation of all kinds] cannot be achieved within capitalism."[108] The inextricable links between capitalism and patriarchy, between class and feminist struggles, that Hennessy and others identify: we can learn from this model (and also from certain recent writings on ecological politics)[109] as we turn to an examination of other forms of identity politics.

There is one final preliminary point to be made, however. This concerns the complexity of grounding morally the resistance to oppression that might link feminist and other movements for equality and justice closely to socialist ones. Just what are we 'moralizing' about in our science, after all? Those on the Left have sometimes shown unease with any such question, preferring instead the assumption of an (at best) tacitly shared hunch as to what positive values might ultimately find expression if "the workers of the world" really were to unite to build a new society. The challenge of postmodernist deconstruction has made it more difficult to let the matter rest there, however. Significantly, some feminist thinkers – Sabina Lovibond, writing against the grain of postmodernist feminism, for example – have confronted the issue head on. Advocating the "global" agenda of an "abolition of the sex class system, and the forms of inner life that belong to it," she defined this programme as being global "not just in the sense that it addresses itself to every corner of the planet, but also in the sense that it aims eventually to converge with those of all other egalitarian or liberationist movements." And the basis of such "convergence"? "The movement should persist in seeing itself as a component or offshoot of Enlightenment modernism, rather than one more 'exciting' feature (or cluster of features) in a postmodern social landscape."[110] Whether, in seeking to resist both relativism on the one hand and liberal/neo-liberal universalism on the other, "the Enlightenment" is the best point of reference for the Left may be open to question, of course. Nonetheless, as Lovibond senses, the problem will not simply disappear. We may find it easier to know what we are against (capitalism and its multiple alienations and oppressions, for example) than to clearly state just what it is that we are for and just what "spaces of hope" we divine – even if concepts like emancipation from oppression and the freedom for self-expression and self-realization, community and equality can be expected to help us define our counter-hegemonic universalism more specifically as we proceed. Perhaps, too, we can affirm that any such "universalism" as we may come to embrace will have to be global in its referent and democratic in the modalities of its emergence. These are, in any case, issues to which we will have to return.

III Marxism: Class and Identity

We can now turn to a brief survey of issues raised for Marxists and socialists by the "identities" highlighted in the volume of the *Socialist Register* for which this essay was originally written (i.e., *Socialist Register 2003: Fighting Identities)*. In doing so, we find ourselves confronted by variables even more difficult to pin down than are those of class and gender, although they are variables with a wide and undeniable range of pertinent effects. We will suggest that none of them can be reduced to mere reflexes of the economic, the material or the class-determined, either for purposes of analyzing oppression or for mobilizing resistance. However, we will see, once again, that Marxists and non-Marxist socialists have every reason to argue that these variables are best treated in close relation to an analysis and a politics of anti-capitalist class struggle. Finally, since the questions broached here are so far-reaching, I will approach them principally on the terrain of global development theory and "third world" struggles that I know best.

(1) Race ... and (Post-)Colonialism

If it is indeed "absurd", as we have seen Bannerji to argue, to ignore the intersection of class not only with gender hierarchies but also with racial discriminations in advanced capitalist settings, then it would be even more foolish to do so when we focus on capitalism as a global system. As Oliver Cox and others have demonstrated, many of the central features we think of as constituting modern racism in the cultural sphere were, in the first instance, shaped in close interaction with the expansion of global capitalism.[111] For this "cultural variable" served both as rationale and booster rocket for "the European consumption of tribal society" which "when viewed as a single process...could be said to represent the greatest, most persistent act of human destructiveness ever recorded."[112] Such a meshing of "race and class" had numerous faces: in driving American imperialism, for example, the vigorous seed of racism planted by the slave trade was complemented fatefully by what Drinnon calls the ideology of "Indian-hating". This, he continues,

> ... reduced native peoples to the level of the rest of the fauna and flora to be 'rooted out.' It reduced all the diverse Native American peoples to a single despised nonwhite group and, where they did survive, into an hereditary caste. In its more inclusive form, Western racism is another name for native-hating – in North America, of "niggers", "Chinks", "Japs", "greasers", 'dagoes", etc.; in the Philippines of "goo-goos"; and in Indochina of "gooks". .... Racism defined natives as non-persons within the settlement culture and was in a real sense the enabling experience of the rising American empire."[113]

Drinnon goes so far as to argue that "in the [American] experience race has always been of greater importance than class, the corner-stone of European property based politics." We may think the dialectic of class and race is rather more complicated than that, but of the impact of "race" *per se* we can have no doubt. Thus, even when the most overtly racist canons of imperial ideology have been self-consciously modified by the Western powers (in order to rationalize the decolonization process of the post-war years, for example), that ideology's central premise of (racial) superiority has tended to be only lightly recast in "moral" terms for both elite and popular consumption. As Furedi notes:

> Increasingly the vocabulary that is applied to the South is morally different from that which is used in relation to the North. Many societies in the South, especially those in Africa, are treated in pathological terms. Africans are routinely represented as devoid of moral qualities.... The new moral equation between a superior North and an inferior South helps legitimize a two-tiered international system.... Race no longer has a formal role to play since the new global hierarchy is represented through a two-tier

> moral system. Gradually, the old silent race war has been replaced
> by moral crusades and by "clashes of civilization".[114]

The latter is, of course, the nether-world of ideology-making inhabited by the Samuel Huntingtons and the Bernard Lewises of the academy. But its public credibility in Western circles can be best gauged by the extraordinary success of Robert Kaplan's recent writings, in which the grimmest possible evocation – a crypto-racist tone, substituting for any real analysis of the structures of global inequality, is central to his work – of Africa's problems ("criminal anarchy", "nature unchecked") is said to capture the essence of today's "bifurcated world".[115]

The sordid reality of global inequality has certainly reshaped the advanced capitalist centres themselves, the impoverished empire having "struck back" (through migration to the metropole) to produce general populations of diverse ethnic and racial composition.[116] Writers like Bonacich and others more recently have explored the split labour markets that this process has produced, and their implications for divided working-class responses to capital.[117] And Stuart Hall and his colleagues have presented, in rich detail, an understanding of some of the cultural/ ideological and political effects of such "racial" diversity, and the complexity of developing counter-hegemonic strategies in advanced capitalist countries that acknowledge this diversity while seeking to encompass and transcend it.[118] My own work, both scholarly and political, on South Africa has also schooled me here. The semi-autonomous but always tightly linked (and shifting) imperatives of class exploitation and racial oppression that have produced both apartheid and a distinctive form of "racial capitalism" there have proven challenging to disentangle analytically. Similarly, consciousness of nation, race and citizenship has often been even more crucial than class consciousness in driving South African resistance. Perhaps the fact that, ultimately, the pull towards (somewhat) colour-blind class relations has produced a grim post-apartheid "false decolonization" along neo-liberal lines may seem like a retrospective vindication of class analysis. But the situation has never been that simple, nor has the politics it demands.[119] In fact, once taken seriously, the irreducible simultaneity of class and race can be seen everywhere to warrant "the forging of alliances between the democratic movement and the labour and socialist movements for multi-racial organization and solidarity rather than sectarianism and chauvinism, and finally ... a strategy that links the struggle for reforms within capitalism with the struggle for its transformation."[120]

However, for the purposes of the present essay let us narrow the focus here (while simultaneously expanding it!) by returning to the wider world and the intersection of class and race in the relationship between the capitalist centre and its periphery. As Biel has argued, "Dependency theory uncovered part of this relationship, essentially the racial capitalism that exists between the North and the South."[121] Of course, we know that the geography of global exploitation has become ever more complicated, the "Third World" now to be found within the First and the First within the Third, such that Hoogevelt can even suggest that "the familiar pyramid of the core-periphery hierarchy is no longer a geographical but a social division of the world economy."[122] And yet things are not yet quite as simple as that either. As Giovanni Arrighi pointed out some years ago (and has reaffirmed, as noted above, in more recent work), the global hierarchy of national economies remains remarkably stable, whatever may be happening to class relationships within those economies: "...the nations of the world", he writes, "are not all walking along the same road to high mass consumption. Rather they are differentially situated in a rigid hierarchy of wealth in which the occasional ascent of a nation or two leaves all the others more firmly entrenched than ever they were before."[123] There is, in short, plenty of evidence of the existence of a global imperial hierarchy, both geographically and socially-defined, that is also "raced" – a kind of "global apartheid", as the point has recently been put.[124]

It is this phenomenon that lies at the heart of recent work carried out under the rubric of "post-colonialism", much of it done in the name of cultural recovery as part of a challenge to the Eurocentric premises of both mainstream and Marxist studies of development and literature. The postcolonial school aims not merely to expose such Eurocentric biases within the global centres of cultural production, but also to listen afresh to those diverse voices of the South that otherwise would be squeezed out of "the canon" and out of global public discourse. Nor is this done principally in the name of "tradition". Acknowledging the impact that Western imperialism and colonialism have had on peoples on the receiving end of that system – whether currently resident in the south or now in one or another diaspora – they speak in terms of "hybridities" and "syncreticisms" that articulate their presence around the world in voices that are complex and multi-layered, local yet global, and that must be heard.

There have also, however, been numerous critics of such preoccupations who attack the tendency of this work to merely celebrate diversity (of "identity" or of literary and artistic production) at the expense of saying nearly enough about how the world actually works for the vast majority of those who live at capitalism's periphery (whether in the North or the South). Amongst the most perceptive of such critics has been Ella Shohat:

> The circulation of "post-colonial" as a theoretical framework
> tends to suggest a supercession of neo-colonialism and the Third
> World and Fourth World as unfashionable, even irrelevant
> categories. Yet, with all its problems, the term "Third World" does
> still retain heuristic value as a convenient label for the imperial-
> ized formations, including those within the First World.... At this
> point in time, replacing the term "Third World' with the "post-
> colonial" is a liability. Despite differences and contradictions
> among and within Third World countries, the term "Third World"
> contains a common project of (linked) resistances to neo-
> colonialisms [and] implies a belief that the shared history of neo/
> colonialism and internal racism form sufficient common ground
> for alliances among such diverse peoples.[125]

While she acknowledges that the use of the term "Third World"
risks blurring "the differently modulated politics in the realm of
culture, the overlapping spaces of inter-mingling identities" in
diverse settings around the world, she nonetheless affirms that
"the cultural inquiry generated by the hybridity/syncreticism
discourse needs re-linking to geopolitical macro-level analysis."[126]

Shohat thus seeks to bring the cultural realities of global
diversity into a strong interface with the realities of global
capitalism and the need to resist it. More recently, Robert Young
has attempted to defend post-colonial theory against such
criticisms by asserting that "many of the problems raised can be
resolved if the postcolonial is defined as coming after colonialism
and imperialism, in their original meaning of direct-rule
domination, but still positioned within imperialism in its later
sense of the global system of hegemonic economic power."[127] This
may be somewhat disingenuous, however. As Arif Dirlik argues,
"postcolonial critics have been largely silent on the relationship
of the idea of postcolonialism to its context in contemporary
capitalism; indeed, they have suppressed the necessity of
considering such a possible relationship by repudiating a possible

'foundational' role for capitalism in history."[128] Moreover, even Young himself professes unease with the term "post-colonial", suggesting his actual preference for the notion of "tricontinenta-lism" to capture even more directly "a theoretical and political position which embodies an active concept of intervention within such oppressive circumstances". Nonetheless, he claims that "postcolonialism" (as he defines it) can still serve the purposes he has in mind, capturing the "tricontinental" nature of Southern resistance to imperialism while remaining sensitive to the sheer diversity of the settings in which such resistance occurs. Indeed this latter sensitivity is presented as being amongst "the fundamental lessons of the Marxism of the liberation move-ments": "The foundational concept here is the critique of eurocentrism and unreflective eurocentric assumptions, and the need to radicalize any politics or economics through constructive dialogue to accommodate the particularities of local cultural conditions."

Are we not here, with Shohat, Young and others, gaining some ground, finding the terms in which we can acknowledge global cultural diversity and the quasi-racial structuring of the present global system (and of resistance to it), while also focussing on the simultaneous centrality of capitalism in driving the latter system's inequities and contradictions? There are two potential problems, however. One is the danger that both Shohat's retrieval of "neo-colonialism" and Young's "tricontinentalism" can produce a too simplistic "Third-Worldism", blurring, in the interests of an anti-imperialist focus, the manner in which class divisions within the Third World must themselves be challenged by progressive forces. Such certainly is the fear of another critic of post-colonial theory, Aijaz Ahmad, who has challenged, in the name of a 'One World' anti-capitalist focus, the very concept of a Third World and who might well be equally uneasy about "tricontinentalism".[129] But this is merely to suggest that the task is an unfinished one: to develop a sensitivity to the realities of "difference" and of race within the global system that can be linked creatively with a class-defined analysis of the capitalist workings of that system.

There is a second ambiguity. Young's formulations tend to paper over a tension amongst the various "tricontinental" theorists he evokes, between those who resist the "modernity" that the global system seems to thrust upon them and others who wish to seize hold of that very modernity, albeit on their own terms, in order to transform their material condition. There is wide gap in this respect between a Gandhi and an Amilcar Cabral, although from a reading of Young you might not know it. What, then, would be the nature of the one world we might seek to build? Surely Marxists (of both Third and First Worlds) would not wish to dismiss altogether the promise of "modernity", even though much of the currently fashionable postmodernist/postcolonial anti-developmental literature invites them to do so. As Sutcliffe – who finds real value in the analytical turn towards "culture" and diversity[130] – nonetheless argues: "The criticism of the standard development model seems at times too total. Because the old destination, which in the West we experience every day, seems so unsatisfactory, all aspects of it are often rejected as a whole. Along with consumerism out goes science. technology, urbanization, modern medicine and so on. And in sometimes comes a nostalgic, conservative postdevelopmentalism."

> In all projects, there is a danger of losing the baby when we throw out the old bath water. In this case the baby is the material, economic, productive basis of whatever satisfactory utopia can be, to echo Vincent Tucker's suggestive words, imagined and democratically negotiated among the inhabitants of earth.... One way of rephrasing all these concerns would be to say that

> development and globalization are experienced in practice in
> conditions of profound inequality of wealth and power between
> nations (imperialism) as well as between classes and sexes
> (capitalist class exploitation and patriarchy). It is necessary to
> distinguish which of the rejected aspects of development and
> globalization are inherent in these concepts and which come
> about because of the unequal circumstances in which we
> experience them. If we reject them completely because of the form
> in which they arrive we will always be struggling against the
> wrong enemy.[131]

One world out of two, three or four, and not the world of
capitalist globalization: here we are clearly being drawn back to
the question of universalism that was posed in the previous
section. Can there be any doubt that the "race-ing" of the actually-
existing world presents a reality autonomous enough in its
workings (if also one rooted in material realities) to be a focus of
political work in its own right? From this point of view, 'anti-racist'
consciousness-raising must surely complement anti-capitalist
mobilization. But, beyond that, what is to be said about the
mobilization of "positive" racial consciousness as part and parcel
of a progressive movement?

This is clearly delicate ground, and it is to the credit of writers
like Paul Gilroy that they have sought to negotiate it. Gilroy is well
aware of the liberatory potential of some degree of racial self-
identification in helping overcome the psychological and material
scars inflicted upon "people of colour" by the malignant workings
of racism.[132] He is also a fierce critic of any too easy evocation of
universalism – as his crisp exposé of the racist stereotypes
underlying Kant's own "Enlightenment values" eloquently
demonstrates.[133] And yet Gilroy also identifies the dangers of a
black "raciology" that, in the name of identity and "the disabling
assumption of automatic solidarity based on either blood or land",
risks merely a narrow inversion of white and racist definitions of

"difference" by black "victims" that liberate no one. Instead he urges, in the name of a "resolutely non-racial humanism", a "fundamental change of mood upon what used to be called 'anti-racism'" by asking it "in an explicitly utopian spirit to terminate its ambivalent relationship to the idea of 'race' in the interest of a heterocultural, post-anthropological and cosmopolitan yet-to-come."[134]

Not all militants, black or white, will agree with this way of posing things. Many Marxists, for example, will wish to ground their pursuit of "utopian" goals more firmly in terms of class struggle than Gilroy's brand of "humanistic voluntarism" seems to promise.[135] Following Sutcliffe's distinctions, they may also want to qualify Gilroy's premise that, for victims of capitalism, "corrective or compensatory inclusion in modernity should no longer supply the dominant theme."[136] And yet, at the same time, race does matter: Marxists must seek to avoid all traces of smugness as we accept the assistance of Gilroy and others across the racial divide. For his attempt to "imagine political culture beyond the colour line" does help stake out terrain upon which the continuing effort to synthesize diverse resistances to oppression can occur.

(2) Ethno-nationalism and Religion

Another challenging front for Marxists is that of "ethno-nationalism". Attempts to define precisely the attributes, shared and distinctive, of nation/nationalism, ethnic group/ethnicity, tribe/tribalism, and other related terms have filled hundreds of combative volumes. For present analytical purposes, the term "ethnie" may help us to link all these notions: as defined by Anthony Smith, "ethnie" refers to a community "which unites an emphasis upon cultural difference with the sense of an historical community. It is this sense of history and the perception of cultural uniqueness and individuality which differentiates populations from each other and which endows a given population with a definite identity, both in their eyes and in those of outsiders."[137] It has become a commonplace to recognize that such "communities" are imagined, and even willed into active existence by class-defined protagonists and political actors, but that does not make the often long-lived histories and cultural attributes thus evoked entirely arbitrary. Nor does it make irrelevant the variable circumstances under which a sense of difference cast in such terms can become politicized, nor make less real the effects of actions taken by people (often in large numbers) in terms of such identities, as the last several centuries of history have made perfectly apparent. Marxists have been understandably troubled by this phenomenon, as ethnonational claims have cut across class identities and consciousnesses in wildly varying ways, so much so that Tom Nairn once famously argued that "the theory of nationalism represents Marxism's great historical failure."[138]

Not that Marxists need apologize for their profound suspicions of ethno-nationalism: an emphasis on "inter-nationalism as the expression of a revolutionary humanist viewpoint" and on "socialist, democratic and emancipatory alternatives to national exclusivism, chauvinism and xenophobia" is at the core of their perspective.[139] We have, in recent months, supped full of the United States' Great Power chauvinism and Israel's own brutally self-righteous project (both being defined at the grisly intersection of racism, nationalism and religious pomposity, as these things so often are); and we have scarcely recovered from the "ethnic cleansings" of ex-Yugoslavia and Rwanda (to cite only two of the grimmest recent cases). But, as Ronaldo Munck has asked, is this pull towards "the tribe" always and everywhere to be interpreted by Marxists as mere "problem", or should it not instead be treated as "an integral element of the human condition"[140] – as being, quintessentially, one of those "different empirical circumstances/historical influences" referred to by Marx that affect "the economic basis" in ways that can be "ascertained only by analysis of the empirically given circumstances"? Thus even Lowy, citing the range of manifestations of nationalism, from Nazism to the Vietnamese revolution, is prepared to emphasize "the contradictory role of nationalism"; to define it as being, in fact, "one of the great paradoxes in the history of the twentieth century".[141]

Something similar can also be said of religious identities. Perhaps most Marxists may be atheists, comfortable enough with a materialist perspective on the transcendental and the "last things"; this is certainly true of the present writer. They may even edge towards what Bryan Turner has termed "reductionist" approaches to understanding the realm of the religious – tending to see religion "as an epiphenomenon, a reflection or expression of more basic and permanent features of human behaviour and society", with the further implication that "religious beliefs are false by reference to certain scientific or positivistic criteria and that the holding of religious beliefs is irrational by reference to criteria of rational thought."[142] But is there any need for Marxists to be so reductionist? Our very silences regarding issues of death, evil and enchantment will seem to many quite one-dimensional. Surely people can be encouraged to find their own workable "truths", spiritual or otherwise, regarding such issues. In sum, there seems no reason for Marxists to feel they must advocate "existential materialism" to others, and, quite apart from the unlikelihood of succeeding in doing so,[143] there are many reasons not to even attempt it.[144]

Once again, then, it is not religious belief, but the way in which religion is institutionalized, politicized or "classed", that should concern Marxists. And here there are good reasons to be suspicious. Once again, Michael Lowy asks the most pertinent of questions: "Is religion still, as Marx and Engels saw it in the nineteenth century, a bulwark of reaction, obscurantism and conservatism? Is it a sort of narcotic, intoxicating the masses and preventing them from clear-sighted thought and action in their own interests?" To which he replies: "To a large extent, the answer is *yes*."[145] And yet Lowy, in the very book in which he writes these words, is primarily concerned to evoke the reality of "liberation theology" (which he terms "liberationist Christianity") and the positive ways in which it has come to frame certain contestations for radical space in Latin America, including, most recently, in Chiapas. This reality, too, suggests that there is work to be done by Marxists and socialists in better comprehending and acting upon the world's complexities.

Note that Lowy then proceeds to document the extent to which a significant tradition within Marxist theory has actually been alert to such issues. Both Marx and Engels, he argues, acknowledged the role that religion could play both in defining political hegemony and in inspiring political protest.[146] And Lowy also praises the efforts of Rosa Luxemburg "to rescue the social dimension of the Christian tradition for the labour movement ... [i]nstead of waging a philosophical battle in the name of materialism." True, "Luxemburg's insight, that one could fight for socialism in the name of the true values of original Christianity, was lost in [the] rather crude and somewhat intolerant 'materialist' perspective"[147] prevalent in the Marxist circles of the time. But he can also cite Gramsci, Bloch and Goldmann as Marxist writers who countenanced the possibility of a creative (if contested) interface between the utopianism and faith principles in both Marxism and religious belief.[148] For Lowy, the Peruvian Marxist José Carlos Mariategui is particularly central in this respect[149] – not least in influencing directly the work of his fellow Peruvian, the founder of liberation theology, Gustavo Gutiérrez. For, as noted above, it is in the emergence of liberation theology that Lowy identifies most clearly "the appearance of religious thinking using Marxist concepts and inspiring struggles for social liberation [and] the creation of a new religious culture, expressing the specific conditions of Latin America: dependent capitalism, massive poverty, institutionalized violence, popular religiosity."[150]

Of course, Lowy is well aware that this is contested terrain in Latin America as elsewhere; his analysis of the virulent reaction against liberation theology by the established Catholic church in Latin America (and in Rome) and the interests clustered behind it, as well as the American-sponsored offensive of evangelical Protestant missionaries on that continent, is usefully sobering, as is his discussion of tensions within the camp of the liberationists themselves (with some, not surprisingly, being much more Romantic and/or populist than Marxist). Still, it is the possibility of a progressive articulation between religion and popular-cum-class struggle that bears primary emphasis here. As Dwight Hopkins also concludes, "religions embodied in disparate human cultures have served as the foundations for national differences, racial conflicts, class exploitation, and gender discrimination, on the one hand, as well as for the resolution of hostility and the achievement of full humanity for those at the bottom of all societies, on the other."[151]

Cannot something similar be said for "ethno-nationalism"? The initial prognosis is not promising, as noted above: ethno-nationalist perspectives easily lend themselves to the purposes of great power chauvinism and the rationalization of bourgeois interests for popular consumption in wealthy countries. Moreover, "the pitfalls of national consciousness" (in Fanon's phrase[152]) are familiar in poorer countries where they often mask petty-bourgeois in-fighting over power and serve to "divide and rule" popular forces in the interests of elites, warlords and their sponsors. But even as we move to re-pose the next obvious question – why do large numbers of ordinary people, especially in impoverished circumstances, become available for the narrowest, most combative kind of mobilization in such terms? – we must pause. For, as Munck writes, "The critique of nationalist discourse should not blind us to the popular struggles it has [also] fostered and animated. ... The struggles of the subaltern may take many forms – nationalist, ethnic, regional and religious amongst others – and a marxism that seeks to have global influence needs to understand these and not just struggle to 'demystify' them and reassert a 'true' class struggle."[153]

For the Marxist there will be two key foci here, the claims of universalism/internationalism on the one hand and the diverse modalities of "articulation" between ethnie and class (just as between religion and class) on the other. Once again, the Marxist tradition does have helpful contributions to draw on, an internationalism that has been open to a diversity of struggles (including those cast in national terms) while also emphasizing their "indivisible interdependence", in Trotsky's phrase.[154] Both Lowy and Munck cite Otto Bauer as advancing "a concept of the nation as historical process of rich and subtle historical analysis", and acknowledge the contributions of Gramsci as well in this regard.[155] In my own work I have found the early formulations of Laclau – written before his post-Marxist turn – to be particularly helpful.[156] For here one finds a non-reductionist model that rejects the notion that nationalism belongs to any class and insists instead (through the deployment of case-studies of 1930s' Germany and Peron's Argentina) that it can be articulated with quite diverse class projects. More work certainly needs to be done along these lines – not least in the light of the argument of Ahmad, Panitch and others that, despite globalization, the nation-state will remain crucial to the struggle for radical outcomes. For if the latter point is true, the challenge of imagining, on the left, a nationalism that is at once inclusive (with reference to difference), expansive (with reference to internationalism) and progressive (with reference to class) will persist.

It should be apparent from our earlier argument that a similar approach can also illuminate the political economy of religion. As noted, some Marxists may wish merely to challenge religion's "irrational" claims root and branch (as the Frelimo leadership chose to do in Mozambique) or, faced with religion's often negative articulation with class and power, merely to urge an assertive commitment to secularism and to "tolerance" as being the Left's optimal programme. And yet even this latter approach, if pushed too smugly, can easily overlook the kind of potentially positive articulations between religion and class that many situations may actually demand and that "liberation theology" exemplifies.[157] Certainly, making links with those who are moved by the universally humane themes in the world's religious traditions must often be the correct approach by the Left to such a powerful, virtually inevitable, form of identity. In short, religion must not be abandoned to the Right. Here we can take our lead from Dussel's sense that liberation theology "will be practiced in other parts of the Christian world, such as Africa and Asia [beyond Latin America], and by theologians of other world religions. ... This theological perspective emerges from a commitment to the poor of the South, that is, those who have been excluded from the present globalization modernizing process."[158] It is in this spirit, too, that Radhika Coomaraswamy, writing on recent developments in Sri Lanka, refuses to elide the distinction between Buddhist humanism and Buddhist chauvinism and then argues more generally (she comments on Hinduism, Islam and Christianity in addition to Buddhism) that "all religions have this contradiction between orthodox doctrine and the humane heterodox traditions." Herself a secularist, she nonetheless suggests that "to collapse humanism and orthodoxy at this historical juncture would be a major setback."[159]

And yet we must also face the fact that it will be uphill work to claim the high ground here. Recent studies have recognized not merely the vested interests that can benefit from stoking the fires of various fundamentalisms (cf. Islam in the political economy of contemporary Iran, Pakistan, Bangladesh and elsewhere, for example; Buddhist "radicalism" and its links to Sinhala chauvinism in Sri Lanka; or the tight mesh in India [and Nepal] of the Hindu Right with "reactionary modernism" as epitomized by US imperial hegemony and by repressive "Hindu nationalism" – not to mention the resonance of the Christian Right in the United States which so helps fuel all of the horrors perpetrated by Bush and company from there). But they have also emphasized the morbid global conditions that can encourage ordinary people to see such identities, both for better and for worse, as weapons in their own hands. In this sense, Dussel's phrase, "globalization modernizing process", as a touchstone for progress suggests problems of its own. For many students of the religious Right have found the latter's main roots to lie not so much in exclusion from modernity as in resistance to it. Thus, Karen Armstrong, a particularly subtle and sensitive writer on world religions, can underscore the extent to which the fundamentalist version of religious activism is an unsurprising effect of the disruptions that "modernity" brings, and of the fact that "in the developing world... modern Western culture [is experienced as] invasive, imperialistic and alien."[160] Similarly, Mark Jurgensmeyer writes that "in many cases, especially in the areas of the world where modernization is a synonym for Westernization, movements of religious nationalism have served as liberation struggles against what their supporters perceive to be alien ideologies and foreign powers."[161] Faith and fundamentalism, humanism and secularism, universalism and modernity: self-evidently, the complexities evoked by engaging such expansive terms outrun the limits of these pages. What can be insisted upon here, however, is that "modernity" must not be identified as readily with capitalism as Armstrong and Jurgensmeyer (however tacitly) both seem prone to do. Contemporary socialists must insist (once again, with Sutcliffe) that the promise of the modern can be blended with the integrity of the local and the sacred in much more meaningful and efficacious ways than the "universalism" of *capitalist* modernity (Benjamin Barber's "McWorld"[162]) can ever hope to allow.[163]

The question therefore returns: is not *socialist* advance a key piece of the puzzle of building a different, more positive kind of universalism? I would suggest that this is the way the issue should now be framed, with Marxists forced to see the fever so often attendant upon rabid ethno-nationalisms and religions-turned-fundamentalist as a reflection not merely of the victory of capitalism but also the failure, at least for the moment, of "progressive nationalism and revolutionary socialism throughout the globe." As Panitch elaborates the latter point, "Opposition to capitalism and imperialism is inevitable, but the atavistic form it took on 11 September can only be understood in terms of what, on that day, tragically filled the vacuum of the 20th century Left's historic defeat."[164] And what, in addition, can be said of the nature of capitalism's "victory"? As Arrighi reminds us, it has primarily been a victory for the continuing hegemony of capitalism's vicious irrationality – a victory scarred by inequality and the dramatic failure to realize the "developmentalism" that system has so often promised.

Indeed, it is the latter failure that has sown so many of the seeds of contemporary decay, producing "a crisis which is most clearly visible in the rise of Islamic fundamentalism in the Middle East and North Africa but is apparent in one form or another throughout the South".[165] For capitalism's grossly uneven development across the world has produced, as Ralph Miliband once put it, "extremely fertile terrain" for the kind of "pathological deformations" – predatory authoritarianisms and those "dema-gogues and charlatans peddling their poisonous wares ... of ethnic and religious exclusion and hatred" – that now scar the global landscape.[166] Losing confidence in socialist and other humanely modern, humanly cooperative, projects, people turn for social meaning to more ready-to-hand identities, often with funda-mentalist fervour.[167] Despite this, progressives committed to class struggle should continue to view the identities we have been exploring as contingent in their socio-political implications and, in many cases, as not being in contradiction with socialist purposes. And we should continue, when possible, to invite the bearers of such identities to be partners – alongside feminists, environmentalists, anti-racists, activists around issues of sexual orientation, and the like – within a broader community-in-the-making and within a universalizing democratic project of global, anti-capitalist transformation.

*   *   *

This remains the bottom-line. Yes, Marxists and other socialists are themselves ensnared in discourse; but it is a discourse – a "moralizing science", a "point of view", an "entry-point" – of class analysis and class struggle that is user-friendly, meaningful and important to us, and one that, politically, can be rendered important to many others. And not, I would suggest, as folded into the melting pot of diverse oppressions, diverse resistances, diverse movements, under such rubrics as "radical democracy", but as articulated – non-reductively, non-economistically, non-Eurocentrically, but centrally – with them. For Marxist and other socialist discourses imply a crucial demand, a demand to transcend the structural and cultural limits of capitalism that is too easily lost to view, not only by post-modernists but also within the commonsensical hegemonies and glib universalisms that currently haunt us. It is a discourse that is both central to human emancipation and essentially non-co-optable either by liberalism or reformism. Of course, the demands Marxist/socialist discourse encompasses are corruptible, as history has demonstrated, but that is another, if by no means irrelevant, story. Here let us merely affirm that, at bottom, class-based politics and anti-capitalism are too central to the cause of human emancipation to be drowned in "difference", however sensitive we must be to the latter's claims. Struggle along such lines – at once methodological and practical – must continue.

THE STRUGGLE, INTELLECTUAL
AND POLITICAL, CONTINUES

In this essay I integrate into the text several "working papers" that, written for the purpose of encouraging the ongoing intellectual and activist undertakings of committed scholars and practitioners in both the "South" and the "North", can serve to focus our attention on a number of crucial development-related themes, especially as regards the African reality. This latter empirical focus is chosen, of course, because the chief ground of my own developmentalist praxis has been Africa. But it is also the case that these working papers were originally prepared for a Workshop at York University in Canada on the theme, "Africa: The Next Liberation Struggle: Socialism, Democracy, Activism".[168] Nonetheless, they were designed not only to promote further discussion of the African case there, but also to draw from participants more general reflections and debate and to encourage a level of understanding and action better able to comprehend the realities of the contemporary world and to support the actions of the marginalized and exploited everywhere.

Liberation and Democracy

Along these lines, the first working paper sought to focus the theme of "liberation and democracy" and presented the following argument: The languages of both "liberation" and "democracy" have been amongst the most potent over recent decades in Africa, "liberation" (generally cast in terms of "national liberation" in the first instance) driving the dramatic process of emancipation from white minority rule in southern Africa and "democracy" being amongst the most salient of claims advanced by activists and intellectuals contesting the authoritarian states that have blanketed so much of Africa since independence.

In fact, there are few more contested concepts on the terrains of either political science or political practice than these two. For example, while few would deny the importance of the demand for more "democracy" in Africa (or, for that matter, of the often parallel demand for "human rights") the precise meaning and resonance to be attached to such demands is much debated. Particularly suggestive in this respect is a key differentiation made some years ago by Issa Shivji when he distinguished between "liberal" and "popular" democracy.[169] In doing so, Shivji in effect linked his critique of "liberal democracy" to those who have similarly seen that "thin" form as exemplifying "polyarchy" (Dahl and Robinson), "democratic elitism" (Schumpeter), "low intensity democracy" (Gills, Rocamora and Wilson) and "pseudo-democracy" (Phillip Green). And he suggests his preferred alternative – "popular democracy" – to be characterized positively by a much more vibrant form of popular mobilization and empowerment and by "its position on imperialism, state and class, class struggle, etc."

A more widespread realization of even a primarily procedural democracy might represent a step forward in Africa, of course. It could provide fresh space for disciplining from below various all too prevalent authoritarian tendencies, for example, and, in the pursuit of unity, some acceptable mechanisms for reconciling differences, especially those that are "communally defined" by ethnicity, regionalism and religion. For the Left, it could also provide some relatively open political ground upon which to build their own institutions of long-run resistance and transformation. It is no wonder then that demands for the formal guarantees of "bourgeois democracy" in Africa have been prominent on the agenda not merely of the IFIs, international donors and some sectors of the African middle class but also of many popularly-based organizations.

Yet it has proven notoriously difficult to realize even a relatively vibrant liberal democracy in Africa. A situation of extreme scarcity renders the intra-elite struggle over spoils particularly intense. Meanwhile, global pressures to adapt to neo-liberalism narrow the range of options that can easily be articulated by newly "democratic" governments and thus competed over in elections. Popular cynicism and indifference are often the result. Worse, under such conditions quasi-democratic competition can easily become reduced to the lowest common denominator of religious and regional infighting. Moreover, the pull towards renewed authoritarianism under such circumstances is very strong.

The possibility that democratic competition might merely increase fissiparous tendencies in Africa at the expense of national unity and national purpose is what led Nyerere in his time, and Uganda's Museveni more recently, to argue for one-party/one movement regimes (albeit driven by quite different agendas of national purpose: "African socialism" on the one hand; neo-liberal policies on the other). Analysts have often suggested this kind of cure to be far worse than the disease, however. In Tanzania, for example, it sanctioned TANU's drive to not only sideline ethnic politics but also undermine, in the name of unity, the potential for more progressive, popularly-based expressions from independent organizations of workers, women, youth and communities,[170] while in Uganda it helped rationalize Museveni's project of harbouring power to himself and his chosen associates. Indeed, it is difficult to think, in the light of African experience (to go no further afield), that even quasi-benign intentions can overcome the costs to radical politics that the failure to secure an open terrain for the expression of oppositional politics provides. And, of course, the propensity on the part of leaders for political closure are often far more malign than those of a Nyerere or a Museveni.

Such questions become even more salient in the light of the experience of those "successful" movements for liberation that have achieved power in southern Africa. The demand for anti-colonial liberation, as directed against white rule in that region, was an implicitly democratic one, although one that, in practice, often led to more authoritarian practices than any convincing definition of democracy would readily countenance. True, one could see, however briefly, some promise of a "radical nationalism" guaranteeing both a socialist programme and a process of mass empowerment. But even in the best case scenario – as, perhaps, in Mozambique, where revolutionary elites did attempt, at least for a time, to realize policies and programmes designed to better the lot of the masses – the vanguardist failure to really open up the political arena to the potential messiness but also long-term promise of mass politics helped undercut the revolutionary potential of the regime as surely as did the cruel acts of destabilization inflicted upon an independent Mozambique by apartheid South Africa. There more formally democratic institutions, when they came, did help contain some of the internal contradictions that had sustained a cruel civil war but they also produced a polity that, in other ways, drew the population away from any consciousness of shared public purpose that the socialist project had once seemed to promise in that country.

And elsewhere the region witnessed liberations that were even more unambiguously compromised from the outset: Angola, where the increasingly corrupt rule of the MPLA in Angola bent (like Mozambique) under the weight of South African and US destabilization but also under the weight of its own neo-Stalinist preferences; Namibia, where the appearance of a liberal-democratic outcome masked a SWAPO dominance that still reflected the autocratic character of that movement's existence in exile; and Zimbabwe, where a combination of arrogant leadership and neo-liberal pressure led both to an upsurge of popular democratic resistance to the debased rule of Mugabe and his colleagues but also to the reinforcement of the latter's ruthless attempt to retain their control.[171]

In South Africa the realization, in the early-1990s, of a liberal democracy seemed to many a most positive outcome of the anti-apartheid struggle in South Africa. Yet as the ANC embraced ever more uncritically a neo-liberal economic strategy and a narrowly electoral definition of mass politics, the costs of that party's overarching legitimacy (as the chief agent of liberation!) began to become more evident. In the event, the immense popular energies that many felt would carry over from the struggle into a mass politics of transformation in post-apartheid South Africa were contained, even effectively demobilized, by the ANC leadership. The bulk of the population, although now more impoverished than ever, apparently was expected to rest content with being little more than spectators at the intra-elite politicking that swirled above them.

Nonetheless, one of the most promising signals in contemporary Africa is the emergence of popular movements on the ground in South Africa that are increasingly inclined to resist the ANC, its policies and its politics.[172] From the authoritarian degeneration of liberation movements once in power the Left can perhaps learn, for Africa, a lesson that is also increasingly clear from historical experience elsewhere. Self-proclaimed vanguards – whether they be acting in the name of national unity or socialism – are more threat than promise to the grounding of a process of popularly-based, socialist politics. Of course, a simple assertion of the virtues of democracy or a tacit assumption of the likelihood of mass radical spontaneity are not enough. Organization and ideology will remain crucial revolutionary tools: the coordination of local resistances must help these to become much more than the sum of their parts, and there will be a role for leadership to shape mass action even as that leadership must itself be held true to its task by pressure from below. The question of how to build and sustain a transformative politics, both in order to achieve power and to use it effectively once achieved, remains a daunting one.

From the assertions of claims to democracy that have begun to occur recently throughout the continent, the Left in Africa can also learn lessons germane to its long-term project. Democratic demands have resonance certainly: the domestic authoritarianism rampant on the continent sees to that and so too, increasingly, may the self-evidently undemocratic global power system that dictates so many outcomes in Africa. There is a language here to be appropriated, albeit a language that is (as suggested above) also subject to abuse and self-interested manipulation both by local and international players. How best, then, to mould the project of democratization into a truly popular weapon, rather than having it continue to be used, at least as often, as a tool of the elite? Is "popular democracy" enough of a marker to distinguish the broader claims for socio-economic as well as political transformation that must be advanced in its name? If not, how overtly and self-consciously must it blend with the attendant projects of "anti-capitalism" and "socialism" in order to guarantee the seriousness of the project that it seeks to encapsulate?

Finally, the question of how local, national, even continental assertions in Africa – for popular democracy, for socialism – plug into global struggles for the transformation of capitalism and the hierarchies of imperialist power is an especially daunting one. For, self-evidently, it will be difficult for any individual African local community or state to so democratize global capitalism and/or the American imperium as to find sufficient freedom from the pressures such structures assert in order to self-confidently and successfully launch their own transformative projects successfully. The dilemma of how popular democratic struggles can come to be mounted at the various sites of possible contestation – local, state, regional, continental, global – in such a way as to begin to tilt the balance of global power is at least as daunting for Africans as it is for people elsewhere – and perhaps, given the extreme vulnerability of the continent, even more so.

Class and Identity

A second working paper encouraged the workshop to focus on many of the same complex issues evoked in chapter 3, above, seeking to introduce for discussion the theme of "class and 'identity' (gender, race, ethnie)." It proceeded as follows: Defining Africa's major challenge with central reference to the negative manner of the continent's insertion into the global capitalist system, as it seems prudent to do, also implies the granting of a certain analytical centrality to the fact of social class, as both globally and domestically structured. It is true that, however crucial to the discussion of the gross inequalities that scar the continent, any such class analysis is complicated in its own terms. Thus, the relative lack of saliency of any domestic bourgeoisie shifts much of the burden of local class domination to the shoulders of various bureaucratic and political elites. Moreover, the relative weakness of the African proletariat in many countries highlights the importance, in terms of stratification, both of highly differentiated peasantries and a diverse range of urban dwellers – many of them more "marginalized" and "excluded" by capitalism than "exploited" in any straightforward Marxist sense – who live alongside those more formally employed and organized as workers. As Post and Wright have written (as quoted earlier):

> The working out of capitalism in parts of the periphery prepares not only the minority working class but peasants and other working people, women, youth and minorities for a socialist solution, even though the political manifestation of this may not initially take the form of a socialist movement. In the case of those who are not wage labourers (the classical class associated with that new order) capitalism has still so permeated the social relations which determine their existences, even though it may not have followed the western European pattern of "freeing" their labour power, that to be liberated from it is their only salvation.... The objective need for socialism of these elements can be no less than that of the worker imprisoned in the factory and disciplined by the whip of unemployment. These prices are paid in even the most "successful" of the underdeveloped countries, and others additionally experience mass destitution. Finding another path has...become a desperate necessity if the alternative of continuing, if not increasing barbarism is to be escaped.[173]

Certainly, then, exploitation and oppression exist in Africa that are firmly class-defined. Nonetheless, considerable subtlety of analysis is required to make the relevant distinctions, and

considerable political creativity is required to make the tran-
scending of such differentiations the stuff of a viable radical,
class-based politics.

Of course, developing a class politics that can underpin
revolutionary practices and implicate revolutionary goals has
proven to be a far from straightforward matter even in much more
developed regions of the world than Africa, a fact that has given
rise, over the past century, to a range of highly contested general
debates about the nature and promise of proletarian politics. Such
debates are germane here, in particular the challenges posed by
the existence of lines of identity and markers of diverse
oppressions, at play in Africa and elsewhere, that cut across class
structures at any number of oblique angles. As noted in the
previous chapter, Bannerji has underscored the "absurdity" of
attempting to see "identity and difference as historical forms of
consciousness unconnected to class formation, development of
capital and class politics." But in doing so she also emphasizes the
impossibility of considering class itself outside the gendering and
"race-ing" that so often significantly characterize it in the
concrete.[174]

This is most obvious – albeit no more or less so in Africa
than in many other settings – with respect, precisely, to the fact of
gender. The burden of patriarchy (borne across a broad spectrum
of violences directed against women, for example, and highlighted
by differential structures of opportunity) are visible enough. Nor
can there be any doubt that capitalist-induced exploitation and
marginalization are uneven in their gender impact, generally
producing patterns that reinforce the higher price of such realities
that is exacted from women (witness in Africa, for example, the
differential import of structural adjustment programmes). On the
other hand, the mobilization and activism of women has grounded

a struggle that is important in its own right on the continent, how-ever much it may often intersect with simultaneous expressions of class struggle. In sum, the terms of gendering both class analysis and class politics is a work-in-progress in Africa as elsewhere.

Whether, terminologically, gender is a fact of "identity" may be disputed, of course. Generally deemed to fall even more clearly under this rubric are the more "imagined" markers of differen-tiation of race, religion, region, nation and sub-nation ("ethnic groups", "tribe"). Not that the term "imagined" should be taken to imply that the embrace of such categories to identify either a manifestation of oppression or a practice of resistance makes the phenomenon they refer to any less real and tangible. In Africa each of these variables has had pertinent effects, with racism both defining and rationalizing the subordination of Africa right up to the present day, and racial consciousness, emanating from the continent itself, having had countervailing emancipatory effects (albeit sometimes rather ambiguous ones) when it has emerged in such forms as Pan-Africanism and Black Consciousness. And since race is still one marker of social privilege in a country like post-apartheid South Africa the ramifications of that fact can scarcely be expected to disappear very quickly.

Globally, too, the racism underpinning the workings of imperialism and contemporary capitalism's world-wide reach has been cited as helping rationalize the West's continued outward thrust – and also as a factor which, alongside potentially diverse material interests, has made the forging of alliances between subordinate classes, North and South, more difficult to achieve than might otherwise be the case. Meanwhile, reaction from below to such racism has helped encourage a vogue for "post-colonial" studies and other less academic expressions of a racially-conscious sensibility that can serve sometimes to illuminate, sometimes to obscure, the workings of the present global system and the promise of a more universalistic emancipation.

National assertions, albeit most often ones defined with reference of the territorial boundaries inherited from colonialism, have, in Africa as elsewhere, also had meaning – although as often as not rationalizing the domination of new elites (Fanon's "pitfalls of national consciousness") as focusing on ongoing processes of popular emancipation. Nonetheless, Munck writes, "the critique of nationalist discourse should not blind us to the popular struggles it has [also] fostered and animated.... The struggles of the subaltern may take many forms – nationalist, ethnic, regional and religious amongst others – and a Marxism that seeks to have global influence needs to understand these and not just struggle to 'demystify' and reassert a 'true' class struggle."[175] Moreover, any argument regarding the potentially positive role to be played by (necessarily transformed) states in challenging capitalist globalization must find itself flirting, to some degree, with "left nationalism" in advancing its case. And then there are those, like Wole Soyinka, who have emphasized the contribution an achieved nationalism can make to blunting the edge of fissiparous intra-state ethnic and regional rivalry that has been so devastating, not least in Africa.[176]

The distinction between national consciousness on the one hand and ethnic (sub-national) consciousness on the other is not an absolutely clear one and is, in any case, generally made more demagogically than with any real precision. It is also the case that ethnic sentiment, like nationalism more strictly defined, is too often merely mobilized and manipulated by self-serving elites. Still, even Soyinka acknowledges the possible wisdom, when all else has failed, of some ordinary Africans finding solace and sanctuary (of language, kin and territorial affinity) in the most proximate of (ethnic) self-definitions. If the latter tend not to find much in the way of long-term emancipation by choosing such a survival strategy, it is surely the failure of both capitalism and socialism to yet deliver on their promises of a genuinely humane "developmentalism" that must be seen as providing a significant part of the explanation for the vacuum into which these and other far more "pathological deformations" (Miliband) of consciousness enter.

For we exist in a world not only of global capitalism but also of exploding fundamentalisms – in which leaders like Bush and Sharon and many Muslim and Hindu protagonists not only wrap themselves in the flag for purposes of advancing their own schemes of domination but also blur the lines between their national claims and their religious ones. Not that there is any very convincing reason for Marxists to reject, on first principles, the religious impulse that does help many to cope with questions of death, evil and spirituality. Too often socialists in power (in Mozambique for example) have declared war on religion and other identities, rather than find ways to acknowledge the latter's claims to be heard, albeit possibly transformed, within the broader emancipatory project. Moreover, with regard to their implications for revolutionary aspirations, institutionalized expressions of organized religion have proven to be a potent force for both good (one thinks of "liberation theology" in Latin America, for example) and also substantial ill.

Leo Panitch has recently written that "class, as we are so often reminded, is not everything." "But nor", he continues, "is it nothing, and the costs of the marginalization of class in the intellectual and political arena are becoming increasingly severe."[177] If this is so, on the religious front as on other fronts we need to understand a great deal more about the ways in which class analysis and class struggle can, as noted in the preceding chapter, be articulated – non-reductively, non-economistically, non-Eurocentrically (as suggested in chapter 3), but centrally – with other markers of social differentiation, both analytically and practically.

Socialism and Development

What, then, of the "imaginaries" in terms of which people might be expected to mobilize themselves in order to realize more humane and expansive alternatives to the present status quo of existent global capitalism? What, in particular, of socialism in this regard? A third background paper sought, therefore, to introduce this theme of "Socialism and Development" into the Workshop's deliberations, proceeding as follows: The Third World in the 1960s and early-1970s was marked by the growing saliency of "socialism" as an alternative socio-economic system to the capitalism that had underpinned European colonialism and that now drove the United States towards the role of presumptive global hegemon. While by no means the dominant premise throughout the continent of Africa, there was, here as elsewhere, a sense that such an alternative was available, perhaps in particular as an outgrowth of the success of national liberation movements in southern Africa. Alongside these developments in the "real world" the world of scholarship also saw significant commitments to such a prospect both within Africanist circles but also more broadly. By the turn of the century, however, much less was heard of the once-presumed "necessity" of socialist solutions to the problems of underdevelopment that stalked the globe and – perhaps most dramatically – Africa itself.

There is a paradox here. Capitalism as a global system is ever more ascendant, in the wake both of the collapse of the decadent "state socialism" of the Eastern bloc and the aggressive assertion of both its own inherent globalizing tendencies and the political actions of its main protagonist, the United States military machine. And yet the system continues to produce the grossest of inequalities and, for an increasing number, the direst of poverties. The situation might seem, therefore, to cry out more strongly than ever before for the intensified articulation of both a socialist political/economic practice and a socialist-inspired scholarship. The fact that this has not generally been the case, and the implications of that fact, defines one of the key subjects to be explored under this rubric.

Of course, disillusion with the claims to be made on behalf of socialism has had much to do with its failure and/or defeat, both North and South, in the twentieth century. Certainly in most of the global South, and especially in Africa, there has been a strong push (in "the age of structural adjustment", as Bill Freund has termed the waning years of the twentieth century) towards the acceptance of a global framework that seems, nonetheless, merely to deliver growing inequality and ever crueler forms of marginalization and exclusion to most inhabitants of the global South. Now, where there are signs of deep-seated resistance to this system, they are cast at least as often in terms of religious fundamentalism as in terms of the goal of mounting a socialist alternative. For many others, the apparent strength of the global capitalist system seems to dictate the judgment that, at best, it can merely be reformed at the margins (e.g., the OXFAM turn, the Mbeki project) or, perhaps, waited out until the ripening of the system's own internal contradictions (the potentially unsettling nature of China's growing presence in the global economy is sometimes cited in this respect, as is, more generally, the possibility of a global realization crisis) place the possible struggle for alternatives to capitalism more realistically on the political agenda.

Any such disillusion with the socialism project, as indeed with the notion of "development" itself (the other framing term for this section), has been reinforced by the rise of "postmodernist" preoccupations that question fundamentally the status of such "grand narratives" in the name of what are said to be more diverse and localized "truths" and less "Eurocentric" preoccupations. As we have seen Bob Sutcliffe to argue, however, the merits of the goal of development – "the material, economic, productive basis of whatever satisfactory utopia can be imagined and democratically negotiated among the inhabitants of the earth" – must not be lost to a "nostalgic, conservative post-developmentalism".[178] Of course, Sutcliffe would be amongst the first to argue that the material goals of such a "left-developmentalism" must be realized in ways that are equitably distributed, environmentally responsible and democratically defined, but his point stands. A similarly commonsensical claim for the theoretical validity of conceiving a socialist alternative to actually existing capitalism (this latter being, at once "contingent, imbalanced, exploitative and replaceable", in Albo's phrase[179]) can also be made for our present purposes.

In consequence, we will concentrate less on the ontological foundations of socialist preoccupations – and of their link to a drive for meaningful "development" in both material and human terms – than on their practical viability, and this at a number of levels. Even in their own terms, for example, socialist experiments have not found entirely convincing ways to realize long term economic transformation: such is the record in Africa as elsewhere. Perhaps unduly influenced by the Soviet model these experiments have often been disproportionally focussed on high-tech, big project models and on "solutions" to the rural problem that have fetishized collectivism at the expense of genuine local empowerment and planning. Finding (short of seeking to realize an unlikely autarky on a state or regional basis) effective ways to negotiate the choppy waters of the global economy even while working with others to transform its grim logic, and discovering convincing means of blending, domestically, planning and market mechanisms to sustain on-going transformation: there is much to be discussed here regarding the manner, once again in Albo's terms, of "re-embedding financial capital and productive relations in democratically organized national and local democratic spaces sustained through international solidarity and fora of democratic cooperation".

"Democratic cooperation"? Surely the second great weakness of socialists in power in the last century was political, particularly with respect to the authoritarian practices they so often came to adopt. Instead of facilitating the more active expression of organized popular energies (unions, cooperatives, feminist initiatives) such "socialists" proved far more likely to entrap them in an iron cage of vanguardism and ideological correctness. Even their apparently progressive predilections with regard to the transformation of gender roles often calcified in practice, and any necessary sensitivity to the complex bases of religious and other identities proved to be minimal. Not that mere spontaneism provides any effective and convincing answer in the building of an anti-capitalist counter-hegemony. A role for leadership must be acknowledged and defined, but the sustaining of an effective dialectic between such leadership and mass action, with the popular classes checking leadership from below even as they raise their own level of consciousness, must remain as one of the biggest challenges for socialist practice.

Perhaps, then, there are lessons to be learned from prior practice for next time, if and when power is once again attained by socialists. For the moment, however, it is the means – under contemporary conditions and in the wake of such failures – of building movements to win such power that must be at the centre of our discussion. The political critique presented in the preceding paragraph has relevance here: how to avoid the perils of vanguardism and narrow-mindedness in seeking to focus popular energies bubbling up from below. For, despite the residue of disillusion and defeat referred to above, there are such energies, reflected in the stirring of multi-faceted responses to the workings of global capitalism and spawning resistances that have stretched from the global streets of Seattle, Quebec and Genoa, to the national campaigns for political and socio-economic rights, and to the quotidian fight-back of many local communities, groups and trade unions against the inequities they face in trying to build decent lives for themselves and their children.

One suspects that these energies will continue to find expression in the contesting (i) of the deepening exploitation of workers; (ii) of the marginalization and exclusion of vast numbers of people both urban and rural (those who are especially affected by the increasingly Draconian neo-liberal commodification of a wide array of the necessities of life: water, electricity, health, education, housing and the like); and (iii) of the inequitable burden of costs borne in the sphere of social reproduction, not least by women and those racially discriminated against. But how best to conceive the means of pooling such energies at appropriate sites of struggle – local, national, regional, global – and create the effective political tools (of both organization and ideology) to generate an effective, democratic, counter-hegemonic force to capitalist dictate? Gindin, in this regard,[180] has spoken of the "structured movement" ("something transitional that is more than a coalition and less than a party") as a possible step towards what

is needed, and a range of voices, stretching from anarchist to vanguardist, have also been heard from. For there can be little doubt that further developing the theory and practice of a politics of real, not merely notional, revolutionary challenge to the status quo stands as a central task.

And just what kind of counter-hegemony might this political alternative be articulating in any case? The discrediting of socialism as a plausible practice has led to the increased saliency of other imaginaries for grounding the global struggle against inequality. "Radical democracy" is one such alternative that is offered (by Laclau and Mouffe, for example) as a way of acknowledging the multiple fronts on which that struggle might proceed. It is, however, a language that blunts unduly the focus on capitalism and class struggle than seems necessary. A problematic centered on the claims of social justice, has more to offer perhaps, as does the imaginary of "anti-capitalism", this latter much evoked in books and political discourses these days. But just where does that leave the socialist imaginary? Is it a battle-flag too soiled by history to still attract support? Too bad if so, since the socialist tradition is one that, for all its flaws, encourages us to move most efficaciously from a searching critique of capitalism to a potential programme for building its alternative. Does it not seem worth fighting to revive it, if this is indeed the case?

True, even if the goal of a revolutionary socialism ("realistic socialism" as distinct from "utopian capitalism", in Albo's terms) should continue to be seen as providing the most effective foundation upon which to build a real challenge to global capitalism, it is crucial that this imperative not be reduced to mere rhetorical bombast. If "mere reformism" holds no answer, then neither does a jejune "ultra-revolutionism". Instead, we might find instruction in the kinds of revolutionary realism favoured by the early Gorz and by Kagarlitzky, amongst others. Such authors have deployed the notion of "structural reform" to evoke the kind of struggles to realize intermediate victories that, even when pursued and won, keep the long-term goal of ever broader transformation in sight and also further empower the popular classes, organizationally and ideologically, to pursue it.[181] Other related formulations are possible, of course, but on this front, where considerations of strategy and tactics meet the articulation of long-term goals, we also need creative thinking.

Scholar Activism

What then, finally, of the link between intellectual work and anti-imperialist and anti-capitalist activism? A fourth background paper, designed to focus a final session of the Workshop on this theme and therefore defined by the topic "Scholar Activism" argued as follows: Africa has been a regional site where the link between scholarship and activism has been a particularly strong one. Many Africanist scholars from beyond the continent were first drawn to its study by periods of work there and/or by an association with the drama of national liberation struggles, especially those directed against the most calcified examples of white-minority rule in southern Africa. Such scholars often sought to blend their professional work with their activist work around African struggles (the anti-apartheid movement, for example). And much the same could be said, in terms of the impact on a younger generation, of the continuing drama of, and challenges presented by, the African post-colonial crisis – whether this be measured in terms of the dismal economics of structural adjustment, the politics of domestic conflagration, or the grim toll of the AIDS. Not surprisingly, such challenges have been even more important in eliciting the political commitments of a significant section of the African academy as well.

Africa is not alone in this respect, of course. In most settings there are pulls on scholars, particularly those working in the social sciences, to bring their scholarship self-consciously into creative interaction with their political commitments and practices. Indeed, many such scholars will argue that not only is this the only morally appropriate stance that they can adopt, it is also a crucial underpinning of the most effective kind of scientific practice in the social sciences. From some such starting point, we must explore the possibilities and paradoxes inherent in attempting to bring academic undertakings and meaningful political work together, both generally and in terms of the conditions that presently define the situation of the African continent (and other continents of the "global South"), of Canada and other advanced capitalist countries, and of the global capitalist system taken as a whole.

We should not underestimate, nor apologize for, the extent to which the business of scholars who are also dedicated to activism is, in fact, scholarship. Thus scholars (the reference is primarily to scholars of the academy, with the word "intellectual", as Gramsci has reminded us, having a much more expansive connotation) can have the space and time to research, to debate, to raise questions in a particular (somewhat more leisured, at least in some Western settings) way that does not come easily to others more immediately and "practically" engaged. In consequence, they can hope to make a distinctive contribution to the task of discerning a line of march and revealing various problems, possibilities and complexities – always assuming that they sustain a critical self-consciousness about the inevitable limitations of their own perspectives and remain open to as wide a range of voices and experiences as possible. Just what the most appropriate kinds of contribution to struggle that a scholarship cast in these terms might seek to make is, of course, a matter for further discussion.

But if, at least in principle, scholarship has a contribution to make to revolutionary theory and practice, activism (as anticipated above) has an essential contribution to make to scholarship...and to science. For, as Hugh Stretton argued some years ago,[182] "neutral scientific rules" cannot replace "values as selectors" in the framing of the questions that we ask; moreover, the "scientistic" dream of developing an internally coherent, self-sustaining and (potentially) exhaustive model of society is not only misguided but dangerous – dangerous in the sense of encouraging a blunting of debate regarding the diverse "political and moral valuations" that necessarily shape both the questions we pose, as scholars, about society and the explanations that contest for our attention regarding social phenomena. Hence his argument for the self-conscious embrace of what he terms a (necessarily) "moralizing [social] science".

We might wish to add that, once the questions have been posed, social scientists can still be judged by their peers in terms of the data adduced in the attempt to answer them, and in terms of the coherence of the arguments presented in doing so. There are scientific canons of evidence and logic of presentation against which explanations can, up to a point, be judged and evaluated at least somewhat objectively. But as for the questions themselves, and the importance attached to finding answers to one particular set of questions rather than another, this will be determined by choices – by judgments as to appropriate emphasis and focus – of quite another kind. Nor is this realization of the subjective (and inevitably, political) dimension of effective social scientific inquiry something that Marxists should feel uncomfortable with. It is, at one level, what the unity of theory and practice (with, in Kitching's words, its attendant "rationally motivated willingness to act to transform capitalism"[183]) is all about: theories grounded in radical commitments shape our scholarly undertakings and encourage us to discover things scientifically that more conventional, establishment theories merely serve to hide from sight.

Of course, there are dangers attendant upon the activist scholarship that embrace of a "moralizing science" valorizes, including the obvious temptation to shape findings and quasi-scholarly assertions to fit the apparent imperatives of more immediately pressing political loyalties and goals. This can lead, in the researcher, to self-deception, to wilful distortion, or, more subtly, to a distinct temptation to mask advocacy in the language of scientific justification. All scholar-activists will have been accused of such sins at one time or another and, in truth, these failings are difficult to avoid. Here the facilitating of open, critical but comradely, debate within a broader left-scholarly community can act as some safeguard. Moreover, since the proposed alternative of some sternly objective, "scientistic", social science is largely a will of the wisp, at best naive and trivializing, at worst highly ideological in its own right, honestly confronting such complexities involved in realizing an effective scholar-activism remains a challenge for left-academics.

Such issues need further exploration, of course. But even if we arrive at a position which confirms that scholars can unapologetically assert strong reasons, both moral/political and scientific, to blend their particular professional skills with activism, and where activists can be encouraged to draw on the findings of appropriate scholarship to advance their cause, the larger question remains: just where, within the current neo-liberal conjuncture and in a world dominated by global capital, American imperialism and quasi-religious fundamentalism, can the progressive activist, including the scholar-activist, find the best entry-points for radical intervention?

The Struggle Continues

These are questions that will continue to have to be canvassed, of course, questions that turn around issues of site, agency and imaginary (see chapter 2, above). There is, to begin with, the question of the appropriate site for both analysis and action, with claims for the privileging of the local, the national/regional/continental, and the global all being widely trumpeted. Even more challenging for the scholar activist of radical persuasion is the issue of agency, for here real divisions of emphasis, often visible in the political realm, have also penetrated the academia. Thus, against claims made on behalf of class analysis (and a range of variants of Marxist scholarship) one will sometimes find a congeries of oppositional post-modernism, identity politics and an advocacy of local, even spontaneist, initiatives challenging Marxism's erstwhile hegemony on the left, both within the academy and beyond.

Developing a class analysis sufficiently flexible to keep issues of exploitation, marginalization and exclusion at the centre of our preoccupations while acknowledging the range of other oppressions that can both interpenetrate with class and give rise, as "militant particularisms", to resistances in their own right: this presents us with a challenge (as discussed earlier in this chapter). So, too, does the complex issue of arbitrating (and, where possible, blending) the claims of diverse organizational expressions that left impulses can take: the local community vs. the (national) state vs. "global civil society"; the political party vs. the trade union vs. the "social movement" (whether this be premised primarily on considerations of gender, community or identity).

Finally, there is the question of the appropriate imaginary in terms of which we can best advance both left "theoretical practice" in the academy and left practical activism beyond it. There is, for example, the question of the status of Marxism as core analytical framework versus the range of post-Marxisms, neo-Marxisms and anti-Marxisms that contest that status. Even closer to the coal-face of the struggle itself, and as also discussed above, radical democracy, social justice concerns, anti-capitalism (including the sub-sets of anti-capitalist globalization and anti-imperialism), and socialism all stake their claims to primacy, and each has its advocates on the left.

As suggested above, the main focus of the workshop, which the background papers integrated into the argument above sought to help guide, was "Africa: The Next Liberation Struggle?" and an essay on that topic was also registered as a further broad framing paper for the Workshop as a whole. Since this essay serves to focus another, more Africa-centered, volume of writings recently published by the present author[184] I will not seek to reproduce it here beyond noting the promise of its initial paragraph. For, in fact, it sought to bring "into focus the immediate challenges facing progressives in Africa [and in other continents of the global South] as they now seek to forge social and political initiatives that can hope to attain power and implement policies able to confront and ultimately to bend the apparent logic of global capitalism – thereby permitting more humane outcomes...." Taking as a starting-point the moment of heightened reflection on such issues that occurred in Dar es Salaam in the 1960s and early 1970s, the essay sought to update the insights of that period with reference to the even grimmer circumstances in which Africa currently finds itself.

Suggesting that mere "reform" (NEPAD, "liberal democratization") offers little real promise of meaningful and substantial change in the continent's desperate situation, the paper sought to then canvas the range of resistances in Africa that indicate the emergence of a more radical project of transformation. While acknowledging that it is easy to be pessimistic regarding such possibilities, the paper identified sufficient movement on the continent to suggest that Africa, in terms of the emergence of a "post-nationalist, post-neo-liberal" revolutionary politics, now stands at a moment analogous with 1945 when few could have anticipated the speed with which African nationalist movements would win independence for their territories from colonial rule.

And the essay concluded with the argument that, despite its current eclipse, the language and vision of socialism will have to become part and parcel of this continuing revival of Africa's revolutionary endeavours and of its "next liberation struggle". Of course, it is no easier now than it was in 1945 to divine for the current moment the precise parameters of the likely struggle against present day domination. Or to answer the variety of questions that this moment will throw up. For, as Africans, like others elsewhere, seek to forge more effective organizations for resistance, for example, how will their new movements balance the rival claims to centrality of local, national, regional, continental and global sites of struggle in the focusing of their efforts? How will the trade-off of the relative priorities of plausible short-term reform against the necessary claims of long term structural transformation be handled? And (perhaps most importantly of all) in terms of what counter-hegemonic imaginary, or imaginaries, will this 'post-nationalist, post-neo-liberal' be cast?

African activists themselves, like activists elsewhere, will have to be in the front lines in answering such questions. But the undertakings of a new generation of researchers and writers focusing critically, if also supportively, on the kinds of resistances that are necessary to a genuine liberation from capitalist globalization will certainly have a positive role to play.

CONCLUSION
REVIVING DEVELOPMENT THEORY AS CONTINUING ANTI-IMPERIALIST RESISTANCE AND LOCAL REVOLUTIONARY PRACTICE

A final word to these essays can be brief, for the hour is growing late and there is a great deal of work to be done. As we have seen, there is a need clearly to identify both the grim illogic of the present global capitalist system *and* the nature of the daunting, but far from impossible, challenge that confronts all those who would seek to help the globally exploited, the true wretched of the earth, to rally assertively and in their own right. It is these tasks that surely must form the core of any development theory worth its salt in a contemporary global economy and polity of such cruel countenance: theory that can provide the solid basis for further reflection on the imperatives of anti-imperialist resistance on the global front and of meaningfully radical/revolutionary endeavour on a domestic one. In fact, it is *only* these latter two undertakings, broadly defined, which seem worth considering, both scientifically and politically, as "development studies", given the urgency of the present world-wide crisis of poverty and inequality. One is reminded of Adam Przeworski's sour dictum: "Capitalism is irrational; socialism is unfeasible; in the real world people starve – the conclusions we have reached are not encouraging ones." [185] Yes, one wishes to say to Przeworski, but also, very firmly, NO. In Africa, in India, in Latin America, and elsewhere, we, as development theorists and development practioners, need very much more than so defeated a resignation as Przeworski's (and that of others, cited in our introduction) to what increasingly passes for the way of the world.

NOTES

Introduction

1. Giovanni Arrighi, "World Income Inequalities and the Future of Socialism", *New Left Review*, 189 (September-October, 1991).

2. Arrighi, *ibid.*, p. 64.

3. Giovanni Arrighi, Beverley J. Silver and Benjamin D. Brewer, "Industrial Convergence, Globalization and the Persistence of the North-South Divide", *Studies in Comparative Industrial Development*, 38, 1 (Spring, 2003).

4. Giovanni Arrighi and John S. Saul, "Socialism and Economic Development in Tropical Africa", being the first chapter of Arrighi and Saul, *Essays on the Political Economy of Africa* (New York: Monthly Review Press, 1973); see also, in the same volume, chapter 2, "Nationalism and Revolution in Sub-Saharan Africa".

5. Giovanni Arrighi, "The African Crisis", *New Left Review*, 15 (May/June, 2002), pp. 35-6. For an approach that takes more seriously the continuing possibility (not to mention the necessity) of a more radical, socialist response to the capitalist-driven underdevelopment of Africa, see John Saul, *Africa: the Next Liberation Struggle* (Toronto, New York, London and Durban: Between the Lines, Monthly Review Press, Merlin Books and the University of KwaZulu-Natal Press, 2005).

6. Paul Blackledge, *Perry Anderson, Marxism and the New Left* (London: The Merlin Press, 2004).

7. Carlos Vilas, "Is Socialism Still an Alternative for the Third World?", *Monthly Review*, 42, 3 (July-August, 1990), p. 108.

8. Carlos Vilas, "Between Market Democracies and Capitalist Globalization: Is There Any Prospect for Social Revolution in Latin America?" in John Foran (ed.), *The Future of Revolutions: Rethinking Radical Change in the Era of Globalization* (London: Zed, 2003), p. 105.

Chapter 1

This chapter was first published, in much the same form, in David A. Clark (ed.), *The Elgar Companion to Development Studies* (Cheltanham: Edward Elgar, 2005).

9. Giovanni Arrighi (1991), "World Income Inequalities and the Future of Socialism", (see footnote 1, above) pp. 57, 52. For further debate and commentary on this issue including evidence of Arrighi's own shifting position on the implications of such a "global hierarchy" (as also discussed in the introduction to this book) see Giovanni Arrighi, Beverly J. Silver and Benjamin J. Brewer as cited in footnote 3, above; a critical response by Alice Amsden, "Goodbye Dependency Theory, Hello Dependency Theory", *Studies in Comparative International Development*, 38, 1, (2003), pp 32-38; and the reply by Arrighi, Silver and Brewer, "Response", also in *Studies in Comparative International Development* 38, 1, pp. 39-42.

10. See Magnus Blomstrom and Björn Hettne (1984), *Development Theory in Transition: The Dependency Debate and Beyond: Third World Responses* (London: Zed Books, 1984) and Cristóbal Kay, *Latin American Theories of Development and Underdevelopment* (London: Routledge, 1989).

11. Andre Gunder Frank, *Capitalism and Underdevelopment in Latin America*, revised edition (New York: Monthly Review Press, 1969).

12. See Colin Leys, *The Rise and Fall of Development Theory* (Oxford: James Currey, 1996).

13. Frank, *ibid.*

14. Bill Warren, *Imperialism, Pioneer of Capitalism* (London: Verso, 1980).

15. Geoffrey Kay, *Development and Underdevelopment: A Marxist Analysis* (London: MacMillan, 1975), p. 55.

16. Gavin Kitching, *Development and Underdevelopment in Historical Perspective: Populism, Nationalism and Industrialisation* (London: Routledge, 1989).

17. Manfred Bienefeld, "Dependency Theory and the Political Economy of Africa's Crisis", *Review of African Political Economy* 43 (1988), pp. 85-6.

Chapter 2

This essay was first published, in much the same form, in Leo Panitch and Colin Leys (eds.), *Socialist Register 2004: The New Imperial Challenge* (London: Merlin Press, 2003).

18. Although never quite given the prominence it deserves in most standard history books, this process has, nonetheless, been dissected effectively by a number of prominent western historians who provide their books with various suitably ironic titles: see Eric Wolf, *Europe and the People without History* (Berkeley and Los Angeles: University of California Press, 1982); V. G. Kiernan, *The Lords of Human Kind: Yellow Man, Black Man and White Man in the Age of Empire* (Boston: Little Brown, 1969); Sven Lindqvist, *Exterminate All the Brutes* (New York: The New Press, 1998); Richard Drinnon, *Facing West: The Metaphysics of Indian-Hating and Empire-Building* (New York: New American Library, 1980). Of course, this has also been done by "Third World" scholars themselves (who tend to have a similar gift for to-the-point titling): Chinweizu, *The West and the Rest of Us* (New York: Vintage Books, 1975); Walter Rodney, *How Europe Underdeveloped Africa* (London: Bogle-L'Ouverture, 1972); Eduardo Galeano, *The Open Veins of Latin America: Five Centuries of the Pillage of a Continent* (New York: Monthly Review Press, 1973); and Edward Said, *Orientalism* (New York: Pantheon Books, 1978); there is also, more recently, Sophie Bessis, *Western Supremacy: Triumph of an Idea?* (London: Zed Books, 2003). Unfortunately, such history now stands in increased danger of being whitewashed and recycled for purposes of rationalizing the United States' own current bid for imperial legitimacy, one particularly worrying example of this trend being Niall Ferguson's *Empire: The Rise and Demise of the British World Order and the Lessons for Global Power* (London: Allen Lane, 2002), itself linked to a successful television series.

19. Joseph E Stiglitz, *Globalization and its Discontents* (New York: W. W. Norton, 2002), p. 5.

20. From the WTO's 1999 report, *Trade, Income Policy and Poverty*, as quoted in David McNally, *Another World Is Possible: Globalization and Anti-Capitalism* (Winnipeg: Arbeiter Ring, 2002), p. 92.

21. "Three Men Own More Than 48 Countries", *Mail and Guardian* (Johannesburg), September 23, 1998, reporting on the annual Human Development Report of the United Nations; as that UN document continues: "It is estimated that the additional cost of achieving and maintaining universal access to basic education for all, basic health care for all, reproductive health care for all women, adequate food for and safe water and sanitation for all is roughly $40-billion a year. This is less than 4% of the combined wealth of the 225 richest people."

22. See, for overviews, the "Afterword" (entitled "Sustaining Global Apartheid" to Patrick Bond, *Against Global Apartheid: South Africa Meets the World Bank, IMF and International Finance*, Second Edition (London: Zed Press, 2003), Peter Waterman, "The Global Justice and Solidarity Movement" (draft manuscript: forthcoming) and, for a range of diverse examples of concrete struggles, both McNally, *op. cit.* and Philip McMichael, *Development and Social Change: A Global Perspective*, Second Edition (Thousand Oaks: Pine Forge Press, 2000), esp. ch. 7, "The Globalization Project and its Counter-movements". See also Stephen Gill, *Power and Resistance in the New World Order* (Houndmills: Palgrave Macmillan, 2003).

23. Ankie Hoogvelt, *Globalization and the Post-Colonial World: The New Political Economy of Development*, Second Edition (London: Palgrave, 2001), p. xiv.

24. Beverley J. Silver and Giovanni Arrighi, "Workers North and South", in Leo Panitch and Colin Leys (eds.), *Socialist Register 2001: Working Classes, Global Realities* (London: Merlin Press, 2000), 56-7.

25. Giovanni Arrighi, "World Income Inequalities and the Future of Socialism", *New Left Review*, 189 (September-October, 1991), as cited in the introduction to the present volume (see Footnote 1).

26. Giovanni Arrighi, Beverley J. Silver and Benjamin D. Brewer, *op cit.*; the same issue of *Studies in Comparative International Development* (38, 1, Spring 2003) also includes an exchange, cited earlier (footnote 9) between Alice Amsden and the authors which serves, I think, to reinforce the latter's case.

27. Arrighi, *op. cit.*, p. 65.

28. Arrighi, Silver and Brewer, *op. cit.*, p. 26; a similar chasm, albeit one defined over a much longer period of time, separates Arrighi's prognosis for Africa in the 1960s, when (as noted in our introduction), writing with the present

author, he asserted that "socialist construction is a *necessary* means to the end of development in Africa"(in Giovanni Arrighi and John S. Saul, *op. cit.*) from the much more limited possibilities for change he now envisages for the continent in his "The African Crisis", *op. cit.* (footnote 5).

29. See, importantly, Brian S. Smith, *Understanding Third World Politics* (Bloomington: Indiana University Press, 1996), ch. 1, "The Idea of the 'Third World'"; John Toye, *Dilemmas of Development: Reflections on the Counter-Revolution in Development Economics,* Second Edition (Oxford: Blackwell, 1993), ch. 1, "Is the Third World Still There?"; and Fred Cooper and Randall Packer (eds.), *International Development and the Social Scientists* (Berkeley and Los Angeles: University of California Press, 1997), "Introduction".

30. Manuel Castells, *The Information Age: Economy, Society and Culture,* in three volumes (Malden and Oxford: Blackwell, 1996, 1997, 1998).

31. Michael Hardt and Antonio Negri, *Empire* (Cambridge: Harvard University Press, 2000).

32. Leslie Sklair, *The Transnational Capitalist Class* (Malden and Oxford: Blackwell, 2001).

33. Gary Teeple, *Globalization and the Decline of Social Reform* (Aurora: Garamond Press, 2000).

34. James Petras and Henry Veltmeyer, *Globalization Unmasked: Imperialism in the 21st Century* (Halifax: Fernwood Books, 2001).

35. Leo Panitch, "Globalisation and the State", in Ralph Miliband and Leo Panitch, *The Socialist Register 1994: Between Globalism and Nationalism* (London: The Merlin Press, 1994), p. 63, and many of his subsequent writings.

36. Paul Hirst and Grahame Thompson, *Globalization in Question* (London: Polity Press, 1996), p. 189.

37. Colin Leys, *The Rise and Fall of Development Theory* (London: James Currey, 1996), p. 23.

38. Colin Leys, "Africa's Tragedy", *New Left Review*, 204, 1994, p. 46.

39. The most symptomatic works in this vein have been written by Peter Evans, as, for example, his *Embedded Autonomy: States and Industrial Trans-formation* (Princeton: Princeton University Press, 1995), and numerous articles.

40. William Graf, "The State in the Third World", in Leo Panitch (ed.), *Socialist Register 1995: Why Not Capitalism* (London: The Merlin Press, 1995), p. 159.

41. David Plank, "Aid, Debt and the End of Sovereignty: Mozambique and Its Donors", *Journal of Modern African Studies* (1993), 31, 3.

42. Manfred Bienefeld, "Capitalism and the Nation State in the Dog Days of the Twentieth Century", in Ralph Miliband and Leo Panitch, *The Socialist Register 1994: Between Globalism and Nationalism* (London: The Merlin Press, 1994), pp. 122-3.

43. Graf, *op. cit.*, p. 159.

44. Panitch, *op. cit.*, p. 63.

45. There were also other Marxist theorists of "underdevelopment", of course, some of whom chose to see - along classical lines - an unfolding process of global capitalist development that was necessary to produce genuine proletarian-based struggles in the longer run (Bill Warren's "Chicago Marxism", as Fred Bienefeld once termed it, being a central point of reference here).

46. This "counter-revolution" (to both "Keynesianism" and orthodox "structuralist developmentalism") has been well described in John Toye, *op. cit.*, where he skillfully evokes the roles played by the likes of Harry Johnson, Peter Bauer, Deepak Lal, Ian Little and Bela Belassa.

47. Amartya Sen, *Development as Freedom* (New York: Anchor Books, 1999).

48. See, *inter alia*, Jonathan Crush (ed.), *Power of Development* (Londan and New York: Routledge, 1995), esp. ch 11 by Arturo Escobar, entitled "Imagining a Post-Development Era".

49. For a strong statement of the weakness of much development theory in terms of gender see Catherine V. Scott, *Gender and Development: Rethinking Modernization and Dependency Theory* (Boulder: Lynne Rienner, 1995); see also Chandra Mohanty, "Under Western Eyes: Feminist Scholarship and Colonial Discourses" in C. T. Mohanty, A. Russo and L. Torres (eds.), *Third World Women and the Politics of Feminism* (Bloomington: Indiana University Press, 1991) and much subsequent literature.

50. Bob Sutcliffe, "Development after Ecology", in V. Bhaskar and A. Glyn (eds.), *The North, the South and the Environment: Ecological Constraints and the Global Economy* (London: St. Martin's Press, 1995).

51. Bob Sutcliffe, "The Place of Development in Theories of Imperialism and Globalization", in Ronaldo Munck and Denis O'Hearn (eds.), *Critical Development Theory: Contributions to a New Paradigm* (London and New York: Zed, 1999), pp. 150-2.

52. Cooper and Packard, "Introduction", *op. cit.*, p. 4.

53. Frans J. Schuurman, "Paradigms Lost, Paradigms Regained? Development Studies in the Twenty-First Century", *Third World Quarterly*, 21, 1 (2000), p. 14. See also Gillian Hart, "Development Critiques in the 1990s: *Culs de Sac* and Promising Paths", *Progress in Human Geography*, 25, 4 (2001).

54. Leys, *The Rise and Fall of Development Theory*, p. 43.

55. See, *inter alia*, Patrick Bond, *Against Global Apartheid (op. cit.)* and Walden Bello, *Deglobalization* (London: Zed Books, 2002).

56. Originating in his article, "The Coming Anarchy", *The Atlantic Monthly* (February, 1994) and spun out as several subsequent books.

57. Thomas P. M. Barnett, "The Pentagon's New Map: It Explains Why We're Going to War, and Why We'll Keep Going to War", *Esquire* (March, 2003). But this popular article is merely the most public face of this industrious Naval War College-based Doctor Strangelove whose career as consultant to policy-makers can be traced at his web-site: http://www.nwc.navy.mil/newrules/ThePentagonsNewMap.htm.

58. Ben Fine, "The Development State Is Dead: Long Live Social Capital?" *Development and Change*, 30 (1999).

59. See Gerald Schmitz, "Democratization and Demystification: Deconstructing "Governance" as Development Discourse", in D. B. Moore and G. Schmitz (eds.), *Debating Development Discourse: Institutional and Popular Perspectives* (New York: St. Martin's, 1995) and David Moore, "'Sail on, O Ship of State': Neo-Liberalism, Globalisation and the Governance of Africa", *The Journal Of Peasant Studies*, 27, 1 (1999). The often authoritarian and corrupt Third World state is, of course, a problem; it is just not the kind of problem that the IFIs prefer to see it is as being.

60. Robert Biel, *The New Imperialism: Crisis and Contradiction in North/South Relations* (London: Zed, 2000), esp. ch. 11, "Permanent Subordination? Structural Adjustment as Control", pp. 231-2.

61. George Soros, *The Crisis of Global Capitalism* (New York: Public Affairs, 1998) and "The Capitalist Threat", *The Atlantic Monthly*, 279 (1997), p. 48, where he argues the existence of a "capitalist threat" that is causing "intolerable inequalities and instability". Indeed, he writes that "unless [the doctrine of laissez-faire capitalism] is tempered by the recognition of a common interest that ought to take precedence over particular interests, our present system...is liable to breakdown."

62. Paul Krugman, *The Return of Depression Economics* (New York: Norton, 1999).

63. See Stiglitz, *op. cit.*, and for an even more advanced statement as to the need to "start from scratch" in rebuilding more democratic and effective global financial institutions, see the report of Stiglitz's views in *Financial Times*, August 21, 2002.

64. Of course (as also quoted in our conclusion, below) Przeworski, in his *Capitalism and the Market* (Cambridge: Cambridge University Press, 1991, p. 122) goes further, adding to his claim that "capitalism is irrational" the disempowering reflection that "socialism is unfeasible, in the real world people starve – the conclusions we have reached are not encouraging"!

65. For a searching critique of NEPAD, and of the role of the new South African political elite in promoting it, see Patrick Bond (ed.), *Fanon's Warning: A Civil Society Reader on the New Partnership for Africa's Development* (Trenton and Cape Town: Africa World Press and AIDC, 2002).

66. Biel, *op. cit.*; I have also drawn on these arguments by Biel in developing a more detailed analysis of the possible revolutionary prospect for Africa in the essay "Africa: The Next Liberation Struggle", which is chapter 11 in my *The Next Liberation Struggle: Capitalism, Socialism and Democracy in Southern Africa* (Toronto, New York, London and Durban: Between the Lines, Monthly Review Press, Merlin Press, The University of KwaZulu/Natal Press, 2005).

67. Biel, *ibid.*, p. 232-3.

68. Biel, *ibid.*, pp. 242-3.

69. See, *inter alia*, the titles listed under footnote 5, above.

70. For an example of where an extreme emphasis on the appropriateness of a local focus can lead the development theorist see the 'Conclusion' to Hoogvelt, *op. cit.*; but contrast Giles Mohan and Kristian Stokke on the weakness (and possible cooptability) of such a tendency in their "Participatory Development and Empowerment: the Dangers of Localism", *Third World Quarterly*, 21, 2 (2000).

71. Trevor Ngwane, "Sparks in the Township", *New Left Review* 22 (July-August, 2003).

72. See Naomi Klein, *Fences and Windows: Dispatches from the Front Lines of the Globalization Debate* (Toronto: Vintage Canada, 2002).

73. John S. Saul, chapter 3, below.

74. Cf. John S. Saul, "What is to be Learned? The Failure of African Socialisms and their Future", which is chapter 2 of my *The Next Liberation Struggle* (*op. cit.*).

75. Colin Leys, "Colin Leys Replies" [a reply to Jonathan Barker, "Debating Globalization: Critique of Colin Leys"], *Southern African Report*, 12, 4 (1997). I have explored at greater length some of the issues raised in this section of the present essay in my *Africa: The Next Liberation Struggle* (*op. cit.*).

76. Cf. Neil Smith, "What Happened to Class?" *Environment and Planning A*, 32 (2000).

77. See Ronald Munck, *Globalization and Labour: the New "Great Transformation"* (London: Zed Books, 2002); Beverley Silver, *Forces of Labour: Workers' Movements and Globalization* (Cambridge and New York: Cambridge University Press, 2003); and the various essays in Leo Panitch and Colin Leys (eds.), *Socialist Register 2001: Working Classes, Global Realities* (London: Merlin Press, 2000).

78. Ken Post and P. Wright, *Socialism and Underdevelopment* (London and New York: Routledge, 1989), pp. 151-2.

79. I have elaborated this point in chapter 3, below.

80. J. C. Myers, "What is Anti-Capitalism?" in Joel Schalit (ed.), *The Anti-Capitalism Reader* (New York: Akashic books, 2002), p. 34. On "anti-capitalism" see also McNally, *op. cit.*; working along related lines, Amory Starr, in her *Naming the Enemy: Anti-Corporate Movements Confront Globalization* (London: Zed Books, 2000) emphasizes an "anti-corporate" problematic as particularly appropriate for deepening the terms of popular struggle and coordinating radical activities.

81. Cf. Sam Gindin, "Social Justice and Globalization: Are they Compatible?" *Monthly Review*, 54, 2 (June, 2002).

82. Greg Albo, "A World Market of Opportunities? Capitalist Obstacles and Left Economic Policies", in Leo Panitch (ed.), *Socialist Register 1997: Ruthless Criticism of All that Exists* (London: Merlin Press, 1997), pp. 28-30 and 41.

83. Drawing on the work of André Gorz and Boris Kagarlitzky on "structural reform" I have sought to chart a possible course between "mere reformism" and jejune "revolutionism" in my *Recolonization and Resistance: Southern Africa in the 1990s* (Trenton: Africa World Press, 1993), chs. 4 and 5.

84. Albo, *op. cit.*, p. 30; Albo himself suggests, for starters, the need for "more inward-oriented economic strategies" and the devaluation of "scale of production as the central economic objective"(p. 28).

Chapter 3

This essay was first published, in much the same form, in Leo Panitch and Colin Leys (eds.), *Socialist Register 2003: Fighting Identities* (London: Merlin Press, 2002).

85. For ease of argument in the present essay I have tended to elide the terms "Marxist" and "socialist" throughout; however, I am aware that not all socialists will consider themselves to be Marxists, even if it is likely that all Marxists will (like myself) consider themselves to be socialists.

86. E. H. Carr, *What is History?* (New York: Alfred A. Knopf, 1962), pp. 9, 26.

87. Hugh Stretton, *The Political Sciences: General Principles of Selection in Social Science and History* (London: Routledge and Kegan Paul, 1969), p. 141.

88. Gavin Kitching, *Marxism and Science: Analysis of an Obsession* (University Park: Pennsylvania State University Press, 1994), p. 168.

89. Kitching, *ibid.*, pp. 169-70.

90. Lucio Colletti, "Marxism: Science or Revolution" in Robin Blackburn (ed.), *Ideology in Social Science: Readings in Critical Social Theory* (Glasgow: Fontana/Collins, 1972).

91. "I would say", Colletti (*ibid.*, p. 375) argues in this respect, "that there are two *realities* in capitalism: the reality expressed by Marx and the reality expressed by the authors he criticizes."

92. Stephen A. Resnick and Richard D. Wolff, *Knowledge and Class: A Marxian Critique of Political Economy* (Chicago: University of Chicago Press, 1987): "By entry point we mean that particular concept a theory uses to enter into its formulation, its particular construction of the entities and relations that comprise the social totality"(p. 25).

93. Resnick and Wolff, *ibid.*, p. 99.

94. Resnick and Wolff, *ibid.*, p. 281. That this approach can also lead to very soft definitions of capitalism and of anti-capitalist struggle – see J. K. Gibson-

Graham, *The End of Capitalism (As We Knew It)* (Cambridge: Blackwell, 1996) – is worth noting but does not undermine its merits.

95. The quotations are from Laclau's contribution "Structure, History and the Political" in Judith Butler, Ernesto Laclau and Slavoj Zizek, *Contingency, Hegemony, Universality: Contemporary Dialogues on the Left* (London: Verso, 2000), pp. 203, 206.

96. Equally important to our purposes here is Zizek's further elaboration of this point (in Butler, et. al, *ibid.*, p. 321): "The much-praised postmodern 'proliferation of new political subjectivities', the demise of every 'essentialist' fixation, the assertion of full contingency, occur against the background of a certain silent renunciation and acceptance: the renunciation of the idea of a global change in the fundamental relations in our society (who still seriously questions capitalism, state and political democracy?) and, consequently, the acceptance of the liberal democratic capitalist framework which remains the same, the unquestioned background, in all the dynamic proliferation of the multitude of new subjectivities."

97. Kitching, *op. cit.*, p. 68. As Kitching further explains, "The reason is that Marx was, if nothing else, an extremely intelligent man, and economic reductionism is an extremely silly, not to say incoherent, idea in which to believe."

98. Eric Olin Wright, "Giddens' Critique of Marxism", *New Left Review*, 138 (March-April, 1983), p. 24.

99. See, for example, Nicos Mouzelis ("Sociology of Development: Reflections on the Present Crisis", *Sociology*, 22, 1 [February, 1988]) who argues that "the neglect of the political...is the Achilles heel of all development theory", including Marxist theories of development, but also finds in Marxism's potential openness to embracing the tension between "systemic and agency terms" the key to its ability to overcome any collapse into economistic reductionism (pp. 39-40).

100. Karl Marx, *Capital, vol. 3: The Process of Capitalist Production as a Whole* (New York: International Publishers, 1964,), p. 790-1.

101. Himani Bannerji, *Thinking Through: Essays on Feminism, Marxism and Anti-Racism* (Toronto: Women's Press, 1995), pp. 30-1. In a related manner, Joan Acker seeks a "fluid view of class as an ongoing production of gender and racially formed economic relations, rooted in family and communities as well as in the global organization of capital", thereby helping to overcome the way in which 'women's movements and anticolonialism and antislavery struggles' have often been "divorced from class struggle". See her "Rewriting

Class, Race and Gender: Problems in Feminist Rethinking" in Myra Marx Ferree, Judith Lorberg and Beth B. Hass (eds.), *Revisioning Gender* (Thousand Oaks, Calif.: Sage Publishers, 1999), pp. 62-3.

102. Katha Pollitt, "Race and Gender and Class, Oh My!" in her *Subject to Debate: Sense and Dissents on Women. Politics and Culture* (New York: Random House, 2001), pp. 218-219. As she continues: "Everybody sees that now – even John Sweeney talks about gay partnership benefits as a working-class issue – except for a handful of old New Leftists, journalists and mini-pundits who practice the identity politics that dare not speak its name."

103. Lynne Segal, "Whose Left? Socialism, Feminism and the Future", *New Left Review*, 185 (January-February, 1991), pp. 87, 90. Segal is here critiquing, in particular, those former socialist-feminists like Zillah Eisenstein who had begun to abandon the link between socialism and feminism in favour (in Segal's summary) of a feminist politics that seeks to "unite all women...in their specific identity as women."

104. Nancy Fraser, "From Redistribution to Recognition? Dilemmas of Justice in a 'Post-Socialist' Age", *New Left Review*, #212 (July-August, 1995), p. 68.

105. Rosemary Hennessy and Chrys Ingraham, "Introduction: Reclaiming Anticapitalist Feminism" in their edited volume *Materialist Feminism* (New York and London: Routledge, 1997); such authors regret that crucial concepts like "social structure, production, patriarchy and class ... have been dismissed by post-modernist feminists [and by "a flourishing postmodern cultural politics"] in favour of analyses that ... focus almost exclusively on ideological, state, or cultural practices, anchor meaning in the body and its pleasures, or understand social primarily in terms of the struggle over representation" (p. 5).

106. See, for example, Carol A. Stabile, "Feminism and the Ends of Post-modernism" and Martha Gimenez, "The Oppression of Women: A Structuralist Marxist View" (p. 82), in Hennessy and Ingraham, *ibid*.

107. Hennessy and Ingraham, *op. cit.*, p. 11.

108. Rosemary Hennessy, *Profit and Pleasure: Sexual Identities in Late Capitalism* (New York and London: Routledge, 2000), p. 232.

109. Thus Bob Sutcliffe ("Development after Ecology", in V. Bhaskar and A. Glyn [eds.], *The North, the South and the Environment: Ecological Constraints and the Global Economy* [London: St. Martin's Press, 1995]) demonstrates the necessity of developing a progressive politics that is sensitive simultaneously to ecology and to the imperatives of global redistribution: "The only hope

for a radical redistribution towards the future is a radical redistribution away from the rich in the present. If greater equality in the present is one of the traditional concerns of red politics, greater equality between generations is an essential characteristic of the new green politics. But not all reds are yet green; nor do all greens look as if they will become reds. The future of sustainable human development depends on a more thorough mixing of the colours" (p. 255).

110. Sabina Lovibond, "Feminism and Postmodernism", *New Left Review*, 178 (November-December, 1989), p. 28.

111. Oliver Cox, *Caste, Class and Race* (New York: Monthly Review, 1948).

112. Mark Cocker, *Rivers of Blood, Rivers of Gold: Europe's Conquest of Indigenous Peoples* (New York: Grove Press, 1998), p. xiii. See also Sven Lindqvist, *"Exterminate All the Brutes": One Man's Odyssey into the Heart of Darkness and the Origins of European Genocide* (New York: The New Press, 1996).

113. Richard Drinnon, *Facing West: The Metaphysics of Indian-Hating and Empire Building* (New York: New American Library, 1980), p. xvi-xviii.

114. Frank Furedi, *The Silent War: Imperialism and the Changing Perception of Race* (New Brunswick: Rutgers University Press, 1998), p. 240.

115. Robert D. Kaplan, "The Coming Anarchy", *The Atlantic Monthly* (February, 1994). This seems another paradigmatic example of the 'Western Us' being juxtaposed to 'The Others' that Howard Zinn has critiqued so effectively in a recent commentary on the bombing of Afghanistan. See his "The Others", *The Nation* (February 11, 2002).

116. Note, too, the link made by Hannah Arendt (in her *The Origins of Totalitarianism* [New York: Harcourt Brace, 1951]) between the racisms of imperial expansion and that of genocidal anti-semitism (the latter being a racism with a unique historicity of its own, of course) in the German case.

117. Edna Bonacich, "Class Approaches to Ethnicity and Race", in *The Insurgent Sociologist* (Special Issue on "Race and Class in Twentieth Century Capitalist Development"), 10, 2 (Fall, 1980).

118. David Morley and Kuan-Hsing Chen (eds.), *Stuart Hall: Critical Dialogues in Cultural Studies* (London and New York: Routledge, 1996), and Paul Gilroy, Lawrence Grossberg and Angela McRobbie (eds.), *Without Guarantees: In Honour of Stuart Hall* (London: Verso, 2000).

119. See my "Introduction: The Revolutionary Prospect" in John S. Saul and Stephen Gelb, *The Crisis in South Africa*, Revised Edition (New York and

London: Monthly Review Press and Zed, 1986), Harold Wolpe, *Race, Class and the Apartheid State* (London: James Currey, 1988) and John S. Saul "Cry for the Beloved Country: The Post-Apartheid Denouement", *Monthly Review*, 52, 8 (January, 2001).

120. John Gabriel and Gideon Ben-Tovim, "Marxism and the Concept of Racism", *Economy and Society*, 7, 2 (May, 1978), p. 147.

121. Robert Biel, *The New Imperialism: Crisis and Contradiction in North/South Relations* (London: Zed Books, 2000), pp. 131-2.

122. Ankie Hoogevelt, *Globalization and the Postcolonial World: The New Political Economy of Development*, Second Edition (Houndmills: Palgrave, 2001), p. xiv.

123. Giovanni Arrighi, "World Income Inequalities and the Future of Socialism", *New Left Review*, 189 (September/October, 1991), and Arrighi and Beverley Silver, "Industrial Convergence, Globalization and the Persistence of the North-South Divide", paper presented at the American Sociological Association Meetings, Anaheim, CA, August 18-21, 2001.

124. Salih Booker and William Minter, "Global Apartheid", *The Nation* (July 9, 2001).

125. Ella Shohat, "Notes on the 'Post-Colonial'", *Social Text*, 31/32 (1992), pp. 111. See also, in the same issue of *Social Text*, Anne McClintock, "The Angel of Progress: Pitfalls of the Term 'Post-Colonial'".

126. Shohat, *ibid.*, p. 110.

127. Robert Young, *Postcolonialism: An Historical Introduction* (Oxford: Blackwell, 2001), p. 57.

128. Arif Dirlik, "The Postcolonial Aura: Third World Criticism in the Age of Global Capitalism", in Anne McClintock, Aamir Mufti and Ella Shohat (eds.), *Dangerous Liaisons: Gender, Nation and Postcolonial Perspectives* (Minneapolis: University of Minnesota Press, 1997), p. 502.

129. Aijaz Ahmad, *In Theory: Classes, Nations, Literatures* (London: Verso, 1992), esp. ch. 8, "Three Worlds Theory: End of a Debate".

130. Sutcliffe seeks, however, to incorporate these variables "in a way that allows imperialism once again to become an important theoretical concept". See his "The Place of Development in Theories of Imperialism and Globalization", in Ronaldo Munck and Denis O'Hearn (eds.), *Critical Development*

Theory: Contributions to a New Paradigm (London and New York: Zed, 1999), p. 144.

131. Sutcliffe, *ibid.*, 150-2.

132. See also on this subject Mahmoud Dhaouadi, "Capitalism, Global Humane Development and the Other Underdevelopment", in Leslie Sklair (ed.), *Capitalism and Development* (London: Routledge, 1994).

133. Paul Gilroy, *Against Race: Imagining Political Culture Beyond the Colour Line* (Cambridge, Mass.: The Belknap Press of Harvard University Press, 2000), pp. 58-61.

134. Gilroy, *ibid.*, p. 334.

135. On the pitfalls of "humanistic voluntarism", see Gabriel and Ben-Tovim, *op. cit.*

136. Gilroy, *op. cit.*, p. 335.

137. As cited in Liz Fawcett, *Religion, Ethnicity and Social Change* (Houndmills: MacMillan Press, 2000), p. 3.

138. Tom Nairn, "The Modern Janus", *New Left Review*, 94 (November-December, 1975), p. 3.

139. Michael Lowy, *Fatherland or Mother Earth? Essays on the National Question* (London: Pluto Press, 1998), pp. 2, 4.

140. Ronaldo Munck, *Marxism @ 2000: Late Marxist Perspectives* (Houndmills: MacMillan Press, 2000), esp. ch. 7, "Difficult Dialogue: Marxism and Nation", p. 133.

141. Michael Lowy, *Fatherland or Mother Earth?* (*op. cit.*).

142. Bryan Turner, *Religion and Social Theory: A Materialist Perspective* (London: Heinemann Educational Books, 1983), p. 282.

143. As Hopkins writes (in the introduction to Dwight N. Hopkins, et. al. [eds.], *Religions/Globalizations: Theories and Cases* [Durham: Duke University Press, 2001]), "For the majority of cultures around the world, religion thoroughly permeates and decisively affects the everyday rituals of survival and hope. Reflected in diverse spiritual customs, sacred symbols and indigenous worship styles, global religions are permanent constituents of human life."

144. I say this with some feeling in light of my own experience living and working in Mozambique in the 1970s and 1980s when the ruling liberation movement,

Frelimo, paid what seems in retrospect to have been an unnecessarily heavy price in terms of popular legitimacy for eliding a struggle against the overbearing institutional presence of the Catholic Church with an attack on religious sensibility per se.

145. Michael Lowy, *The War of Gods: Religion and Politics in Latin America* (London: Verso, 1996), p. 4.

146. Lowy (*ibid.*, pp. 6-10) reminds us, for example, of Marx's pithy footnote in Capital (volume 1, chapter 1) in which he suggests of the Middle Ages and of Antiquity that "Catholicism there and politics here played the dominant role", albeit in interaction with permissive "economic conditions"; Lowy's discussion of Engels' approach both to Thomas Munzer's millenarianism and to English Puritanism is also instructive.

147. *Ibid.*, p. 12.

148. See also on this subject James Bentley, *Between Marx and Christ: The Dialogue in German-Speaking Europe, 1870-1970* (London: Verso, 1982).

149. Interestingly, Mariategui evokes Sorel as the first Marxist thinker who understood the "religious, mystical and metaphysical character of socialism" (Lowy, *op. cit.*, pp. 18); for Mariategui as postcolonial theorist see Young, *op. cit.*, ch. 15, where he is quoted as advocating that "We must give birth, through our own reality, our own language, to an Indo-American socialism."

150. Lowy, *ibid.*, pp. 5, 31.

151. Hopkins, *op. cit.*, p. 2.

152. Fanon's third chapter, so entitled, of his *The Wretched of the Earth* (New York: Grove Press, 1968) is the crucial text here, and applies to ethnic as well as to national consciousness.

153. Munck, *op. cit.*, p. 135.

154. Lowy, *Fatherland or Mother Earth* (*op. cit.*), p. 55.

155. Munck, *op. cit.*, p. 133.

156. Ernesto Laclau, *Politics and Ideology in Marxist Theory: Capitalism, Fascism, Populism* (London: New Left Books, 1977). For my own early deployment of Laclau, amongst other theoretical resources, to understand the weight and substance of ethnicity in Africa see "The Dialectic of Tribe and Class", ch. 14 in my *State and Revolution in Eastern Africa* (New York and London: Monthly Review and Heinemann, 1979).

157. The dangers to democratic values and practices that the adoption of a hard version of "secularism" represents is argued, albeit somewhat idio-syncratically and not entirely convincingly, in William Connelly, *Why I am not a Secularist* (Minneapolis: University of Minnesota Press, 1999).

158. Enrique Dussel, "The Sociohistorical Meaning of Liberation Theology", in Hopkins, et. al. (*op. cit.*), p. 41.

159. Radhika Coomaraswamy, "In Defense of Humanistic Way of Knowing: A Reply to Qadri Ismail", *Pravada* (n.d.), pp. 29-30.

160. Karen Armstrong, *The Battle for God* (New York: Ballentine Books, 2001), p. 367, although Armstrong's studies do convince her that under various circumstances "many of the ideals of modern Europe would be congenial to Muslims" (p. 59).

161. Mark Jurgensmeyer, "The Global Rise of Religious Nationalism", in Hopkins, et. al. (*op. cit.*), p. 66.

162. Benjamin Barber, *Jihad vs. McWorld* (New York and Toronto: Random House, 1995), p. 222 and passim.

163. This has *not*, of course, been the practice of most socialist modernizers of the past; twenty-first century socialists have much to learn from the mistakes of their predecessors in this respect. Moreover, many real complexities will still have to be confronted: for example, indigenous "modernizers" seeking to introduce liberatory themes of women's emancipation will have their work cut out for them in many cultural contexts, however deftly they proceed.

164. The failure of the Left or its defeat? Something of both, no doubt, although, as Panitch reminds us ("The Meaning of 11 September for the Left", *Studies in Political Economy*, 67 [Spring, 2002], p. 47), "Whatever responsibility the Left must take for this defeat, there can be no doubt about the major role played by American imperium's world-wide suppression of progressive forces" - adding that "one aspect of this was its cynical sponsoring of reactionary religious fundamentalism as a tool against the secular left in that part of the world on which it has now made war."

165. Arrighi, *op. cit.*, p. 40.

166. Ralph Miliband, *Socialism for a Sceptical Age* (London: Verso, 1995), p. 192; see also, on this subject, Manuel Castells, *The Power of Identity* (Malden and Oxford: Blackwell, 1997), esp. ch. 1, "Communal Heavens: Identity and Meaning in the Network Society" and ch. 2, "The Other Face of the Earth: Social Movements against the New Global Order".

167. Thus Wole Soyinka, noting the dictatorial turn taken by once promising nationalisms in Africa, suggests that the populace's retreat to narrower "cultural identities ... is entirely logical". See his *The Open Sore of a Continent: A Personal Narrative of the Nigerian Crisis* (New York and Oxford: Oxford University Press, 1996), p. 139.

Chapter 4

168. The papers which are integrated into this article were originally presented, as background documents, at the Workshop on "Africa: The Second Liberation Struggle", ably organized by Richard Saunders, Carolyn Bassett and Gigi Herbert and held at York University on October 15-18, 2004. Amongst those present were many who presented quite specific "response papers" to these 'working papers". Included among the invitees and participants were Richard Saunders, Robert Drummond, Pablo Idahosa, Linda Freeman, Colin Leys, Darlene Miller, David Pottie, Greg Albo, Himani Bannerji, Marlea Clarke, Leo Panitch, Greg Ruiters, Atu Sekyi-Otu, Sam Gindin, Giovanni Arrighi, Carolyn Bassett, Manfred Bienefeld, Trevor Ngwane, Leander Schneider, Lionel Cliffe, Jonathan Barker, Judith Marshall, Janet Conway, John Loxley, David Moore and Peter Lawrence. A number of their response papers, as well as some syntheses of the workshop's discussions, are available at the Workshop website: www.arts.yorku.ca/african_liberation/. There is also some overlap of argument (although this is kept to a minimum and presented only in summary statement) and citation (as the following footnotes will testify) with the preceding chapters of this book, but the points made in this chapter seem worth emphasizing, even re-emphasizing where, upon occasion, some minimal repetition occurs, and presenting within an integrated framework.

169. Issa Shivji (1991), *State and Constitutionalism: An African Debate on Democracy* (Harare: SAPES, 1991), p. 255. See, in general, his chapters "State and Constitutionalism: A New Democratic Perspective" (chapter 2) and "Contradictory Class Perspectives in the Debate on Democracy" (editor's Epilogue).

170. *The Next Liberation Struggle: Capitalism, Socialism and Democracy in Southern Africa* (Toronto, New York, London and Durban: Between the Lines, Monthly Review Press, Merlin Press, The University of KwaZulu/Natal Press, 2005), chapter 7 ("Julius Nyerere's Socialism: Learning from Tanzania").

171. On Mozambique, Namibia and Zimbabwe, see *ibid*, chapters 4, 5, and 6.

172. For the South African case, see, *ibid*, Section 3.

173. Post and Wright, *Socialism and Underdevelopment*: see footnote 78, above.

174. Bannerji, *Thinking Through*: see footnote 101, above.

175. Munck, *Marxism @ 2000*: see footnote 140 and 153, above.

176. Soyinka, *The Open Sore of a Continent*: see footnote 167, above.

177. Leo Panitch, "Reflections on Strategy for Labour", in *Working Classes, Global Realities: Socialist Register 2001* (London: Merlin Press, 2000), p. 367.

178. Sutcliffe, "The Place of Development in Theories of Imperialism and Globalization": see footnote 51, above.

179. Albo, "A World Market of Opportunities?": see footnotes 82 and 84, above.

180. Sam Gindin, "The Party's Over", Toronto: *This Magazine* (November-December, 1998), p. 15.

181. John S. Saul, *Recolonization and Resistance: Southern Africa in the 1990s* (Trenton: Africa World Press, 1993), chapters 4 ("South Africa: Between Barbarism and Structural Reform") and 5 ("Structural Reform: A Model for the Revolutionary Transformation of South Africa").

182. Hugh Stretton in his invaluable *The Political Sciences: General Principles of Selection in Social Science and History* (London: Routledge and Kegan Paul, 1969), p. 141.

183. Kitching, *Marxism and Science*: see footnote 88, above.

184. See John S. Saul, *The Next Liberation Struggle* (*op.cit.*, footnote 170, above).

Conclusion

185. Adam Przeworski, *Democracy and the Market* (Cambridge and New York: Cambridge University Press, 1991), p. 122.